Children with Parents in Prison

Children with Parents in Prison

Child Welfare Policy, Program, & Practice Issues

Cynthia Seymour
Creasie Finney Hairston
editors

Transaction Publishers
New Brunswick (U.S.A.) and London (U.K.)

This book is printed on acid-free paper that meets the American National Standard
for Permanence of Paper for Printed Library Materials.

Library of Congress Catalog Number: 00–023862
ISBN: 0–7658–0719–X
Printed in the United States of America

Library of Congress Cataloging-in-Publication Data

Children with parents in prison : child welfare policy, program, and practice
issues / Cynthia Seymour and Creasie Finney Hairston, editors.
     p. cm.
   Includes bibliographical references.
   ISBN 0-7658-0719-X (alk. paper)
   1. Children of prisoners—Services for—United States. 2. Children of
prisoners—Government policy—United States. 3. Prisoners' families—
Government policy—United States. 4. Prisoners—United States—Family
relationships. I. Seymour, Cynthia. II. Hairston, Creasie Finney.
HV8886.US C55   2000
362.7—dc21
                                                 00-023862
                                                        CIP

CONTENTS

FOREWORD

This special edition of *Child Welfare* grew out of the Child Welfare League of America *Children with Incarcerated Parents* initiative. The initiative arose in response to the need expressed by CWLA's member agencies, who had begun to see in their caseloads an increasing number of children with parents in prison. With encouragement from Peter Breen, executive director of Centerforce, a CWLA-member agency; with assistance from the Women's Prison Association and the Osborne Association; and with support from The Hite Foundation, CWLA hosted the National Institute on Children of Incarcerated Parents in Washington, D.C., on March 26, 1996. The Institute drew more than 175 child welfare and criminal justice professionals from across the country. Cosponsors included the U.S. Department of Justice's National Institute of Justice, the Council of Governors Policy Advisors, and Centerforce.

The enthusiastic response to the Institute convinced us that the field wanted and needed more information about children whose parents are incarcerated. In 1997, we began offering special workshop tracks on the subject at our national conferences. We also surveyed state child welfare agencies to find out how aware they are of parental incarceration and what programs and services they currently offer. The survey results demonstrated a dearth of responsive policies and services, but an eagerness for information and assistance. With additional support from The Hite Foundation, CWLA is currently developing a handbook for child welfare agencies to help them enhance their services to children and families separated by incarceration.

This special issue of *Child Welfare* on children with incarcerated parents is a natural outgrowth of our efforts in this arena. As our initiative developed and we became more familiar with parental incarceration, we noticed a lack of scholarly research and writing about the impact on children, particularly through the

lens of child welfare. In addition, we wanted to raise the awareness of and provide up-to-date information to the child welfare
community about the effect of parental incarceration on children.
Finally, we wanted to alert the child welfare community to the
good work being done by the advocates and service providers
across the country who have recognized the needs of this unique
population and have developed responsive programs and services. Although most of the programs for this population are too
new to have been evaluated or reviewed, we felt it important to
include some of them because they represent the first steps in
responding to these children and their families, and will serve as
models for those to come.

Children and families have long struggled with the difficulties created when a parent goes to prison. Until recently, though,
parental incarceration has not been recognized as a discrete issue
warranting study and concentrated intervention. It is our hope
that this special issue of *Child Welfare* will raise public awareness
about the impact of parental incarceration on children; stimulate
discussion about how best to meet the special needs of these children and their families; and provide a resource for the child welfare community as it responds to the growing numbers of children made vulnerable by their parents' incarceration.

Children with Parents in Prison: Child Welfare Policy, Program, and Practice Issues

Cynthia Seymour

As the rate at which adults are being incarcerated in the United States escalates, child welfare professionals are encountering growing numbers of children who have parents in prison. Current estimates indicate that as many as 1.5 million children have an incarcerated parent; many thousands of others have experienced the incarceration of a parent at some point in their lives. These vulnerable children face unique difficulties, and their growing numbers and special needs demand attention. Challenges facing the child welfare system as it attempts to work with this population are explored.

Cynthia Seymour, J.D., is General Counsel, Child Welfare League of America.

An estimated 200,000 children in this country have an imprisoned mother and more than 1.6 million have an imprisoned father.[1] With the nation's incarcerated population growing by an average of 6.5% each year [Gilliard & Beck 1998], the number of children with parents in prison will likely continue to increase. Parental incarceration—and the crimes and arrests that precede it—cause chaos in the lives of these children, including traumatic separations and erratic shifts from one caregiver to another. Most children with incarcerated parents live in poverty before, during, and after their parents' incarceration [Johnston 1995a].

The increasing incarceration rate for adult women is particularly foreboding because incarcerated women are often the sole caregivers of their children. Since 1985, the number of women in prison has almost tripled [U.S. Dept. of Justice 1997]. On any given day, more than 100,000 women are being held in this country's jails and prisons [Gilliard & Beck 1998; U.S. Dept. of Justice 1997]. Six percent of women entering prison are pregnant [Beck et al. 1992].

The Scope of the Problem

Although the number of children affected by parental incarceration can be estimated, the true scope of the problem is uncertain because few reliable statistics exist. For the most part, law enforcement does not gather information about the children of arrested adults and correctional institutions do not ask prisoners for specific information about their children. Because there is no specific agency or system charged with collecting data about this population, it is unclear how many children are affected, who they are, or where they live.

In fulfilling its mission to protect vulnerable children and promote family stability, the child welfare system has been and will continue to be significantly affected by the increasing number of children with incarcerated parents. The U.S. Department of Health and Human Services' 1994 National Study of Protective, Preventive and Reunification Services Delivered to Children and Their Families [U.S. Department of Health and Human Services, Children's Bureau 1997] identified "incarceration" as the presenting problem of the primary caregiver in 4% of the cases of children and families who received child welfare services in 1994. Studies suggest that 8-10% of the children of female prisoners and 1-2% of the children of male prisoners are in some form of out-of-home care [Beck et al. 1992; Beckerman 1994; Bloom & Steinhart 1993; Johnston 1995d; Snell 1994]. Many more children with incarcerated parents likely have intermittent contact with the child welfare system.

Although case workers presumably know on a case-by-case basis when children have parents in prison, a 1997 Child Welfare League of America (CWLA) survey of state child welfare agencies confirmed that most state information systems do not capture data about parental incarceration in a way that permits analysis of the information on a systemwide basis [Child Welfare League of America 1998].[2] In the CWLA survey, only 21% of the 38 responding states indicated that their systems capture this information at the intake and assessment phase. Of these states, several clarified that their systems capture the information only under certain circumstances such as when the parent's incarceration is the primary reason for the placement.

Impact of Parental Incarceration on Children

Much of the research on children with incarcerated parents has been methodologically limited. Many of the studies used relatively small samples and inadequate comparison groups [Gabel 1992; Gaudin & Sutphen 1993]. There have been no longitudinal studies following children through different phases of parental incarceration and release [Gabel 1992]. Few studies have em-

ployed standardized assessments of children and almost no research has been conducted through direct contact with children
[Johnston 1995c; Gabel 1992]. Instead, much of the existing research has relied upon self-reporting by incarcerated parents or
caregivers [Gabel 1992; Gaudin & Sutphen 1993; Johnston 1995c].

The existing literature, though scarce, does indicate that children whose parents are incarcerated experience a variety of negative consequences, particularly in terms of their emotional health
and well-being; contact with their parents; and physical care and
custody [Johnston 1995a, 1995c]. The extent to which a child will
be affected by parental incarceration depends on a large number
of variables, including the age at which the parent-child separation occurs, length of the separation, health of the family, disrup-
tiveness of the incarceration, child's familiarity with the placement or new caregiver, strength of the parent-child relationship,
number and result of previous separation experiences, nature of
the parent's crime, length of the parent's sentence, availability of
family or community support, and degree of stigma that the community associates with incarceration [Gaudin & Sutphen 1993;
The Osborne Association 1993].

Emotional and Behavioral Consequences

Most children with incarcerated parents experience a broad range
of emotions, including fear, anxiety, anger, sadness, loneliness,
and guilt [The Osborne Association 1993]. They may exhibit low
self-esteem, depression, and emotional withdrawal from friends
and family [The Osborne Association 1993]. They may also begin
to act out inappropriately, become disruptive in the classroom,
or engage in other antisocial behaviors [Gabel 1992]. Often, their
academic performance deteriorates and they develop other
school-related difficulties [Gabel 1992]. These emotional and behavioral difficulties have been linked to a variety of factors, including the stress of parent-child separation, the child's identification with the incarcerated parent, social stigma, and attempts
to deceive children about their parents' incarceration [Gabel 1992].

The extent to which these difficulties are tied to factors apart from the incarceration itself—such as poor parenting or the criminal behavior of the parent—has not yet been explored.

Lack of Contact

Approximately one-half of incarcerated parents do not receive any visits from their children; the others receive only infrequent visits [Snell 1994]. Inhibiting visits are such factors as the geographical location of many prisons, the family's inability to afford transportation, the unwillingness of caregivers to facilitate visits, visiting rooms that are inhospitable to children, and parents' reluctance to have contact [Bloom 1995]. Maintaining contact through phone calls and letters is somewhat more common [Snell 1994]—but these forms of communication are limited by a family's ability to afford expensive collect phone calls and by the literacy level of the parent, child, and caregiver.

Physical Care and Custody

Children whose mothers are incarcerated often experience disrupted and multiple placements. Approximately half of children whose mothers are incarcerated live with grandparents, one-quarter live with their fathers, and the remaining one-quarter are placed in out-of-home care or live with other relatives or friends in informal placements [Snell 1994]. These children are often separated from their siblings and may experience erratic shifts in caregivers [Johnston 1995a]. Their new caregivers tend to have low incomes and may lack the social supports and other resources necessary to meet the children's complex needs [Bloom & Steinhart 1993; Dressel & Barnhill 1994].

Parental Incarceration and Child Abuse and Neglect

Parental incarceration may be a risk factor for child abuse and neglect [Gabel 1992].[3] Prior to incarceration, a parent's criminal justice involvement may be symptomatic of family problems or issues that prevent the parent from providing appropriate care.

During a parent's incarceration, children may be at risk if placed with caregivers who are unwilling or unable to provide appropriate care. When a parent is released, the stresses associated with community and family reintegration may also increase the risk of abuse or neglect [Hairston & Lockett 1985].

Children in the Child Welfare System Whose Parents are Incarcerated

Given the general scarcity of information regarding children whose parents are incarcerated, it is not surprising that little is known about children in the child welfare system who have parents in prison. In several ways, children with incarcerated or criminal justice-involved parents are quite similar to the rest of the child welfare population: (1) their families struggle with an array of complex problems, including poverty, domestic violence, inadequate housing, lack of education, and difficulties with interpersonal relationships; (2) children of color are disproportionately affected; and (3) parental substance abuse plays a large role in many of their lives.

It is tempting to characterize these children as no more or less vulnerable than other children receiving child welfare services, but they are different in ways that make them and their families a challenging population to serve. At a minimum, children in out-of-home care with parents in prison have unique permanency planning needs because the length of the parent-child separation cannot be shortened or affected by the parent's completion of a service plan or demonstrated ability to care for the child. These children may also have unique therapeutic needs resulting from the criminal behaviors exhibited by their parents prior to incarceration, the trauma of parent-child separation, or the significant stigma associated with incarceration. In addition, these children have unique casework needs because the structure of the criminal justice system makes it difficult for parents, children, caregivers, and case workers to maintain contact with one another and to plan for the child's future.[4]

Due to the scarcity of reliable data, the child welfare community lacks critical pieces of information about how children are affected by their parents' incarceration and what services and attention they need to increase their overall well-being. It is not known when or why these children come into care—as a result of abuse or neglect prior to the parent's incarceration, as a direct result of the primary caregiving parent's arrest, or as a result of inadequate caregiving arrangements during a parent's incarceration. It is unclear to what extent the problems experienced by these children are attributable to the incarceration itself—and the resultant parent-child separation—or are more closely tied to factors such as poverty, parents' criminal behaviors, and/or inability to provide appropriate parenting prior to incarceration. Little is known about the effectiveness of child welfare interventions, outcomes of child welfare services, or whether these families reunify successfully after the incarcerated parent is released. There are also questions concerning the quality of care for children during their parents' incarceration.[5]

The Current State of Child Welfare Policy and Practice

Although child welfare case workers are seeing increasing numbers of children with parents in prison, few child welfare policies and procedures have been developed. Smith and Elstein [1994] focused on collaboration among law enforcement, child protection, foster care, and correctional services when a primary caregiver is arrested and incarcerated. They contacted 500 child welfare, law enforcement, and correctional officials in 100 counties across the country. Although more than half of the child protective services sample reported increased requests in recent years for help in placing children whose parents had been arrested, 80% acknowledged that there were no specific policies in place for responding to these requests. Similarly, more than half of the foster care administrators reported an increase in the number of children of incarcerated mothers needing placement in family foster homes, but 97% reported that their agencies had no specific policies in place to guide their work with these children.

CWLA's 1997 survey of state child welfare agencies [Child Welfare League of America 1998] confirms that while certain state and local agencies have begun to focus on children with incarcerated parents, few child welfare agencies have enacted policies or developed programs that specifically address their needs. Only six of the 38 responding states reported having policies that focus specifically on children with incarcerated parents.

Twenty-eight states provided information about programs and services available to children with parents in prison. Most indicated that they facilitate visits between incarcerated parents and their children. Twelve states assist parents with prerelease planning; four states provide support groups for children of incarcerated parents and their caregivers; one state offers counseling services for children; and one state works with prison social workers to provide coordinated services for children and parents. Ten states collaborate with other organizations to provide services to children with incarcerated parents.

Only two of the 38 states responding provide their staff with specific training regarding the needs of children with incarcerated parents and only one of these has developed a formal training curriculum.

Shared Interests: Child Welfare's Interface with the Criminal Justice and Prisoner Advocacy Communities

As the child welfare and criminal justice systems increasingly encounter many of the same families, identification of shared interests and collaboration among the different stakeholders becomes imperative.

Child Welfare and the Criminal Justice Community

The child welfare and criminal justice systems have a shared interest in maximizing opportunities for families involved with both systems. If both systems collaborate effectively, the period of incarceration can actually provide an opportunity for positive intervention with families at risk [Women's Prison Association 1996]. Just as incarceration is a symptom of more complex family problems, it also provides an opportunity for assessment of at-risk children and families, identification of broader family issues, and comprehensive intervention. Both systems have a stake in collaboration because effective intervention with incarcerated parents may decrease the likelihood that the parent will reoffend and improve the chances that children will be reunited safely with their parents or find permanency with other families in a timely manner.

Child Welfare and the Prisoner Advocacy Community

The child welfare and prisoner advocacy communities have a shared interest in supporting children and families affected by incarceration. For many years, advocates for prisoners and their families have worked hard to raise awareness about the issue of parental incarceration and to advocate for services directed toward children and families of prisoners. This community's work has focused most intently on the trauma of parent-child separation, the need for parent-child contact, and the threat of termination of parental rights. Although prisoner advocates have long sought to engage the child welfare community concerning parental incarceration, the discussion has seemed to be limited to facilitating visits and working effectively with parents in prison. The child welfare community may have more to offer by contributing to the dialogue its expertise in caring for children who are separated from their parents and its understanding of the need that children have for a permanent family.

Challenges for the Future

The increasing rate of parental incarceration poses a unique challenge—and raises many questions—for the child welfare system. To meet this challenge—and best serve the needs of these children and families—the field should consider creating a comprehensive strategy that includes developing and promoting a research agenda; identifying and addressing the therapeutic needs of children with incarcerated parents; clarifying the role of child protective services; promoting the accessibility of family preservation and support services; developing better methods for facilitating visits and other parent-child contact; enhancing work with children, parents, and caregivers; identifying and addressing the special permanency planning needs of this population; and developing methods for collaboration with the criminal justice system.

Developing and Promoting a Research Agenda

To fully understand the needs of children with incarcerated parents, the child welfare community will need to promote and undertake quantitative and qualitative research on the effect of parental incarceration on children. Ideally, this research will include sufficient sample size, employ adequate comparison groups, gather information directly from children, and follow subjects for a substantial length of time. Important questions to explore include:

- How many children in care have incarcerated parents? Criminal justice-involved parents? How many children are already in care before a parent's arrest? Why did those children come into care? How many come into care because of parental incarceration? With whom do these children live? To what extent is parental incarceration a risk factor for child abuse and neglect?
- To what extent does parent-child separation resulting from

incarceration harm children? To what extent do children find more stability when parents are incarcerated? Are children stigmatized by parental incarceration or has the experience of incarceration been normalized in our society?

- What are the life experiences of children with parents in prison? How does a child's experience of parental incarceration vary with age and developmental level? How does visiting parents in prison affect children?
- What are the permanency outcomes for children with parents in prison? What percentages are reunited with parents, placed permanently with relatives, freed for adoption, or age out of the foster care system? Are children who have been reunited with formerly incarcerated parents safe and well? Do children who are not reunited with parents find stability and permanent families? Can children find permanency with other families and still maintain connections with incarcerated parents? What is the relationship between permanency outcomes and factors such as length of incarceration, number of times a parent is incarcerated, and reasons for the incarceration? Do outcomes differ for children with incarcerated mothers and children with incarcerated fathers? How?
- What child welfare interventions are successful?
- Are programs that keep criminal justice-involved parents and their children together (e.g., prison nurseries, alternatives to incarceration, halfway houses, residential drug treatment facilities) good for children?

Addressing the Therapeutic Needs of Children with Incarcerated Parents

How do the therapeutic needs of children with incarcerated parents differ from the needs of the rest of the child welfare population? If children are traumatized by a parent's criminal behavior, arrest, or resultant incarceration, what are appropriate therapeutic interventions? What interventions work well with young children? School-age children? Adolescents? How can child welfare professionals help children cope with the stigma of parental incarceration? How can child welfare professionals address the special needs of these children without further stigmatizing them?

Clarifying the Role of Child Protective Services

Some experts argue that children become inherently vulnerable when a parent is arrested or incarcerated and that child protective services (CPS) should have an automatic, formalized role in evaluating placement decisions. Others argue that arrested parents should be entitled to make caregiving decisions for their children and that extensive CPS involvement will result in unnecessary placements into out-of-home care.

When a parent is arrested or detained, what role should child protective services play? How can law enforcement and CPS work together most effectively to ensure the safety of children whose parents are arrested or detained? Can community-based organizations play a role by offering voluntary services that support child and family well-being? How can community-based interventions be made more available and accessible?

Promoting Family Preservation and Support Services

A large population of children who may not be known to the child welfare system may be at risk of abuse or neglect because of their parents' criminal behavior and/or incarceration. For those children who are living with parents who are involved with the criminal justice system, family preservation services may help stabilize the family. During a parent's incarceration, children living with caregivers who are overwhelmed or lack resources to meet their needs may benefit from accessing voluntary family support services. Family support services may also help parents who have been released from prison and who are seeking to reunify with their children.

How can preventative services be made more available to families affected by criminal behavior or incarceration? Is there a way to provide family preservation services to families when parents are sentenced to an alternative to incarceration programs? What is the best way to make family support services more accessible to kinship families caring for children with incarcerated parents? What role can community-based organizations play in providing preventative or supportive services?

Facilitating Visits and Other Forms of Contact

Child welfare workers are legally mandated to facilitate parent-child visits when such visits are not detrimental to the child. Visiting can decrease the stress of separation, enable children to maintain relationships with parents, and increase the likelihood of successful reunification. Facilitating visits between children and parents in prison, though, can be difficult. Case workers have identified a number of obstacles to visiting, including inadequate information about visiting procedures, lack of cooperation from departments of corrections, difficulties in scheduling visits, the time-consuming nature of visits, visiting procedures that are uncomfortable or humiliating, concern about children's reactions to visits, and parents, foster parents, or kinship caregivers who are resistant to visits [Women's Prison Association 1996].

Given the extent to which child welfare agencies must manage high caseloads with limited resources, what procedures can help workers facilitate parent-child visits when a parent is in prison? How can workers help children and families keep in touch when parents are incarcerated at facilities far from where the children reside? When parents are incarcerated in facilities that are not hospitable to children? When caregivers are reluctant to facilitate visits? When incarcerated parents or their children express an unwillingness to visit? Is there a role for community-based organizations in facilitating visits and other forms of parent-child contact?

Working with Children, Incarcerated Parents, and Caregivers

Working with Children. With little information and few resources available, what guidance can be given to child welfare professionals working with children who have parents in prison? How should workers explain parental incarceration to young children? How can workers prepare children for prison visits? How can workers help children and caregivers cope when children return from visits? What are the issues surrounding parental incarceration for infants? For small children? For school-age children? For adolescents? For young adults? How can workers help older children sustain relationships with parents who are incarcerated for long periods of time? Is it possible for infants and small children to develop meaningful relationships with parents who are incarcerated for long periods of time? What is the best way to identify and address behavioral issues resulting from a child's experience of a parent's criminal lifestyle or subsequent incarceration?

Working with Incarcerated Parents. Incarcerated parents who hope to reunify with their children must be able to complete their service plans and maintain meaningful contact with their children while they are in prison. For many incarcerated parents, case workers are their only link with children in care. Parents often express frustration about not receiving communication from case workers and not having sufficient information about their children [Beckerman 1994]. Parents also maintain that they are unable to access in prison the services necessary to complete their service plans.

As part of their legal mandate to make "reasonable efforts" to reunify families, case workers are obligated to facilitate contact between parents and their children and to help parents access those services that might allow them to parent their children appropriately upon release. The challenges, though, of maintaining contact with and providing services to parents in prison are great. Geographical distance, prison security requirements, and high caseloads impede case worker communication with parents. And though case workers may recognize a parent's need for drug treatment, job training, education, or parenting classes, they often have little knowledge of services available inside the prison or have difficulties linking parents to available programs [Women's Prison Association 1996].

Given geographical distance and other constraints of incarceration, how can workers better maintain contact with incarcerated parents? How can workers help parents feel connected to their children? How can workers develop service plans that are about more than visitation and that utilize services available to incarcerated parents? How can child welfare and corrections officials develop linkages that facilitate parents' access to services and programs inside the prison?

Working with Kinship Families. Given that most children of incarcerated mothers live with grandparents or other relatives, how can child welfare agencies better support these kinship families? How can workers evaluate risk to children placed in kinship families? How can workers talk with kinship families about the permanency needs of children and permanency options such as guardianship or kinship adoption, particularly when families may be feeling protective and supportive of the imprisoned parent? How can workers engage kinship families in long-term planning, especially when parents will be incarcerated for long periods of time? How can workers help kinship families address their own feelings toward the incarcerated individual? How can workers help kinship families facilitate parent-child contact, particularly when families are angry with the incarcerated individual?

Working with Nonrelative Foster Families. Many nonrelative foster families express concerns about parental incarceration. They question the parenting capacities of incarcerated parents, the likelihood of rehabilitation, and the advisability of parent-child visitation in a prison setting. They may be reluctant to take children to visits because of their own fears about prisons or because of worries about children's reactions to the prison environment.

How can child welfare agencies better support foster families caring for children with incarcerated parents? How can workers support foster parents in identifying their own fears and biases about crime and incarceration? How can child welfare agencies train foster parents to help children understand and cope with parental incarceration? How can agencies help foster parents facilitate contact between incarcerated parents and their children?

Finding Permanency for Children with Incarcerated Parents

Identifying Permanency Needs. Given what is known about child development, a child's sense of time, and a child's need for a safety, security, and consistent, sustaining relationships, what should permanency look like for children with incarcerated parents? What are the permanency needs of infants? Young children? Older children? Adolescents? How can a child's need for permanency be reconciled with a parent's lengthy prison sentence? How can workers evaluate the nature of the parent-child relationship and the extent to which parents and children are bonded? How long is too long for children to wait?

Evaluating Parents' Ability to Provide Permanence. Although one of the most practical considerations in a permanency determination is the length of time a parent will be incarcerated, case workers often find it difficult to obtain the most basic information about a parent's actual sentence, eligibility for parole or expected release date [Women's Prison Association 1996]. Once a release date is established, the fundamental consideration becomes the parent's ability, upon release, to provide appropriate care for a child. In a prison setting, though, it can be difficult to assess parental capacity to support and nurture a child because prison surroundings prevent observation of parent-child interaction in a day-to-day setting. Another important consideration is parental ability to cope with the inevitable difficulties that will be experienced upon release. Case workers may find it hard to predict whether parents will be able to find a job, find housing, cope with financial difficulties, or avoid drug or alcohol relapse.

What practices can be developed to help workers better assess parent-child relationships—and parental ability to provide care and support for children—when parents are incarcerated? How can incarcerated parents demonstrate the competencies necessary to support a decision to reunify? In making permanency decisions, how should workers factor in a history of recidivism? What does concurrent planning and casework look like when parents are in prison? How can workers talk with parents, especially those incarcerated for long periods of time, about the permanency needs of their children? How can workers engage parents in planning for their children's future?

Identifying Other Permanency Options. When reunification is not the appropriate plan for a child, other options for permanency should be considered (i.e., adoption, guardianship, or, as a last alternative, long-term foster care). Because many children with incarcerated mothers are living with grandparents or other relatives, advocates may tend to dismiss adoption as a viable option. While some kinship families may be reluctant to adopt because adoption requires supporting a termination of parental rights proceeding against a family member, other kinship families may welcome the stability that adoption provides. When lengthy incarceration is the primary factor preventing reunification—and the incarcerated parent desires and is capable of sustaining a relationship with the child—open adoption may be a means of preserving that relationship while providing the child with a permanent family. When adoption is not appropriate, guardianship can be a middle ground that provides some security and stability for a child, assigns rights and responsibilities to the caregiver, and still preserves the incarcerated parent's parental rights.

When parents are incarcerated, how do permanency determinations differ for infants, young children, older children, and adolescents? How can all permanency options be explored and discussed with children, parents, kinship families, foster families, or potential adoptive families? When and how can workers talk to parents about voluntary relinquishment, open adoption or other options that provide permanence for children but still allow parents to maintain relationships?

Legal Issues. Parental incarceration does not alter the requirements of state and federal laws, and recommendations for enhanced services to children with parents in prison and their families must be addressed within the existing legal framework. Case workers are legally obligated to make "reasonable efforts" to reunify families separated by incarceration—and courts may hold agencies legally accountable for maintaining ongoing communication with parents in prison and exploring fully the extent to which services might be provided to incarcerated parents [*In re Sabrina N.* 1998]. More than 25 states have termination of parental rights statutes or adoption statutes that explicitly pertain to incarcerated parents [Genty 1995], though, and under the federal Adoption and Safe Families Act of 1997 (P.L. 105-89), children must have a plan for permanency within 12 months of placement.

What must agencies do to meet their legal obligation to work with incarcerated parents? Are incarcerated parents at risk of having their parental rights terminated inappropriately because of permanency timeframes? Or will children linger for inappropriately long periods in care because workers are unable (because of a parent's incarceration) to meet the criteria necessary for terminating parental rights? Given its focus on shorter and more structured permanency planning timeframes, what impact will the Adoption and Safe Families Act have on permanency planning with incarcerated parents? Will states interpret and implement the federal law in a way that will make it harder for incarcerated parents to be reunited with their children?

Collaborating with the Criminal Justice System

The child welfare and criminal justice systems work with many of the same families. At this time, however, the two systems lack formal channels of contact and have not developed methods for information-sharing or coordination of services. Professionals in both systems express frustration about this lack of coordination and acknowledge that increased collaboration between the two systems would certainly enhance outcomes for children and families. Collaboration is difficult, though, because the two systems have different priorities and responsibilities; neither may have a thorough understanding of the other's processes or concerns, and both are often overextended and have limited resources to invest in collaboration.

A few child welfare agencies have begun to engage in collaborative work with state and local departments of corrections. For example, one state agency provides local departments of social services with a contact person at each correctional facility to coordinate visits and services. Another agency has assigned a social worker to a women's prison to act as a liaison for crises involving parents and children. A third state agency assigns specialized staff to cases in which women give birth while incarcerated. In other creative collaborations, child welfare agencies have worked cooperatively with corrections officials to establish eligibility for community treatment programs, collaborated with community service providers to arrange counseling for families and special recreational activities for children, and collaborated with state prisons to establish special facilities for parent-child visitation [Child Welfare League of America 1998].

A needs assessment initiated by the Maryland Department of Human Resources in 1996 provides one model for child welfare agencies wishing to explore collaborations with the criminal justice community [Women's Prison Association 1996]. The initial project activities included collecting background information about parental incarceration in Maryland; convening a focus group of child welfare case workers and managers to discuss their experiences working with incarcerated parents and their children; and visiting Maryland prison and detention centers to understand how facilities, processes, and programs impact child welfare goals and to begin building more collaborative relationships between Maryland's child welfare and corrections officials [Women's Prison Association 1996].

What are the different values underlying the child welfare and criminal justice systems? What shared goals can be identified? How can child welfare and correctional systems gain greater awareness of each other's systems, programs, resources, responsibilities, and concerns? Given the different priorities and responsibilities of each system, to what extent can professionals be expected to collaborate and work together around parental incarceration? What is the best way to develop linkages? To what extent would enhanced outcomes for children translate into beneficial outcomes for the criminal justice system? What specific steps can be taken to facilitate collaboration between the child welfare and criminal justice systems?

Conclusion

As the country's most basic support for vulnerable children, the child welfare system must begin to address the needs of children with incarcerated parents in a thoughtful, systematic way. The articles in this special issue of *Child Welfare* further explore the phenomenon of parental incarceration and its impact on the child welfare system and the children it serves, and present models and first steps toward meeting the needs of these children and families.

Notes

1. No one knows for certain how many children in this country have an incarcerated parent. Extrapolating from data collected in previous studies, the Center for Children of Incarcerated Parents has developed a formula for calculating these numbers: To estimate the number of children with incarcerated mothers, multiply the number of currently incarcerated women by .75 (the average percentage of incarcerated women with children) and then multiply that number by 2.4 (the average number of children per incarcerated mother). To estimate the number of children with incarcerated fathers, multiply the number of currently incarcerated men by .56 (the average percentage of incarcerated men with children) and then multiply that number by 2.0 (the average number of children per incarcerated father) [Johnston 1995c]. Using this formula with 1995 data, 113,100 incarcerated women [U.S. Department of Justice 1997] have 203,580 children and 1.4 million incarcerated men [U.S. Department of Justice 1997] have 1.6 million incarcerated children.

2. In August 1997, the Child Welfare League of America (CWLA) surveyed state child welfare agencies to learn more about the field's level of awareness and state of knowledge regarding children with incarcerated parents. CWLA asked agencies if they could identify the number of children in their caseloads with parents in prison and if they had collected any data around this population. Overall, the 38 states that responded were able to provide almost no substantive data on the children in their systems who have a currently incarcerated parent or a parent with a history of incarceration [Child Welfare League of America 1998].

   Of the five responding states that were able to provide any data at all about children with parents in prison, only one was willing to estimate the number of children in its entire child welfare system with an incarcerated parent. That state estimated that 22% of its child welfare population had a parent in prison. Five states gave figures for the number of children in foster care with an incarcerated parent, but only one of those states was able to give an unqualified number. That state reported 12% of its foster care population had a parent in prison. Two other states were able to provide numbers only for those children who entered foster care because of parental incarceration. Those two states reported that 1.6% - 4% of their foster care populations entered care because of parental incarceration. The remaining two states could provide only estimates. One state estimated that 10% of its foster care population had a parent in prison and the other state estimated that 29.5% of its foster care population had a parent in prison.

In 1993, Virginia surveyed 17 local departments of social services for information about parental incarceration [Virginia Commission on Youth 1992]. With its response rate capturing 49% of the state's total foster care caseload, Virginia reported that 7% of its children in foster care had an incarcerated parent. Twenty-two percent of those children were placed in foster care because of parental incarceration.

3. Data from two recent Child Welfare League of America (CWLA) studies support a potential link between parental incarceration and child abuse and neglect. The Odyssey Project is an ongoing CWLA study of children in residential group care, group homes, and therapeutic foster care [Curtis et al. 1998]. Recently released data show that of the 1,492 children studied to date, 241 (16.2%) have a mother who has been convicted of a criminal offense; 189 (12.7%) have a mother who has served time in prison or jail; 360 (24.1%) have a father who has been convicted of criminal offense; and 309 (20.7%) have a father who has served time in prison or jail. Of the 485 children whose mother and/or father had been convicted of a criminal offense, 36.7% had been sexually abused, 47.0% had been physically abused, and 58.1% had been neglected. These percentages of abuse and neglect are greater than those for the population of children studied who had neither a mother nor a father convicted of a criminal offense—22.9% of whom had been sexually abused, 37.4% of whom had been physically abused, and 22.4% of whom had been neglected. Although the children in residential care or therapeutic foster homes tend to have more serious problems than children in the child welfare population at large, these data are still significant in seeking to understand the extent to which parental incarceration is a risk factor for child abuse and neglect.

    Another CWLA study sheds additional light on the link between parental incarceration and child abuse and neglect. In a study of young juvenile offenders in Sacramento County, California, CWLA worked with community partners in child welfare, law enforcement, and juvenile justice to better understand the overlap between the child welfare and juvenile justice systems [Child Welfare League of America 1997]. The study focused on 9- to 12-year-old children. Of the 75,000 9- to 12-year-olds in Sacramento County, 1.4% (1,026) were known to the child welfare system because of an investigation of child abuse or neglect. In a 175-person randomly selected sample of those 9- to 12-year-old children investigated by child welfare, 18% had at least one incarcerated parent. Of the 132 9- to 12-year-old children who had been arrested in Sacramento County during that year, 50% (66) were known to child welfare. Of those 66 children, 45% had an incarcerated parent. The study also examined the 20 most expensive placements in the Sacramento County child welfare system and found that 90% of those children had an incarcerated parent. Again, these statistics are from a small sample taken from one county's child welfare system—and the study itself did not focus on parental incarceration. Still, the data suggest that the child welfare community should be cognizant of a parent's criminal behavior and/or incarceration as risk factors for child abuse or neglect.

4. A few studies have focused on the difficulties related to permanency planning for children whose parents are incarcerated. One study showed that 78% of incarcerated

mothers seeking to reunite with their children felt that the services they were receiving from public child welfare agencies were inadequate [Johnston 1995b]. Another study found that a major impediment to effective permanency planning may be the lack of contact between imprisoned mothers and case workers [Beckerman 1994].

5. A 1993 study compared the quality of care being provided to children in informal kinship care because of their mother's incarceration with the quality of care provided by nonrelative foster parents [Gaudin & Sutphen 1993]. Based on information gathered from a very small sample (N = 40), researchers concluded that, on several measures, foster families provided a somewhat higher quality of care than extended families, especially to preschool-age children. The measures utilized in the study included the HOME Inventory, the Adult-Adolescent Parenting Inventory, and the Social Network Assessment adapted from Pattison's Psychosocial Network Inventory.

References

Beck, A., Gilliard, D., Greenfeld, L., Harlow, C., Hester, T., Jankowski, L., Snell, T., Stephan, J., & Morton, D. (1992). *Survey of state prison inmates, 1991.* Washington, DC: U.S. Department of Justices, Bureau of Justice Statistics.

Beckerman, A. (1994). Mothers in prison: Meeting the prerequisite conditions for permanency planning. *Social Work, 39,* 9–14.

Bloom, B., & Steinhart, D. (1993). *Why punish the children? A reappraisal of the children of incarcerated mothers in America.* San Francisco, CA: National Council on Crime and Delinquency.

Bloom, B. (1995). Imprisoned mothers. In K. Gabel & D. Johnston (Eds.), *Children of incarcerated parents* (pp. 21-30). New York: Lexington Books.

Child Welfare League of America. (1997). *Sacramento County Community Intervention Program (Findings from a comprehensive study by community partners in child welfare, law enforcement, juvenile justice, and the Child Welfare League of America).* Washington, DC: Author.

Child Welfare League of America. (1998). *State agency survey on children with incarcerated parents.* Washington, DC: Author.

Curtis, P. A., Papa-Lentini, C., Alexander, G., & Brockman, C. (1998, May). *The Odyssey Project: A descriptive and prospective study of children and youth in residential group care, group homes, and therapeutic foster care.* Unpublished data available from Child Welfare League of America, Washington, DC.

Dressel, P., & Barnhill, S. (1994). Reframing gerontological thought and practice: The case of grandmothers with daughters in prison. *The Gerontologist, 34*, 685-691.

Gabel, S. (1992). Children of incarcerated and criminal parents: Adjustment, behavior, and prognosis. *Bulletin of the American Academy of Psychiatry Law, 20*, 33-45.

Gaudin, J., & Sutphen, R. (1993). Foster care vs. extended family care for children of incarcerated mothers. *Journal of Offender Rehabilitation, 19*(3/4), 129–147.

Genty, P. (1995). Termination of parental rights among prisoners: A national perspective. In K. Gabel & D. Johnston (Eds.), *Children of incarcerated parents* (pp. 167-182). New York: Lexington Books.

Gilliard, D. K., & Beck, A. J. (1998). *Bureau of Justice Statistics bulletin: Prison and jail inmates at midyear 1997.* Washington, DC: U.S. Department of Justice, Bureau of Justice Statistics.

Hairston, C. F. (1995). Fathers in prison. In K. Gabel & D. Johnston (Eds.), *Children of incarcerated parents* (pp. 31–40). New York: Lexington Books.

Hairston, C. F., & Lockett, P. (1985). Parents in prison: A child abuse and neglect prevention strategy. *Child Abuse & Neglect, 9*, 471-477.

Johnston, D. (1995a). The care and placement of prisoners' children. In K. Gabel & D. Johnston (Eds.), *Children of incarcerated parents* (pp. 103–123). New York: Lexington Books.

Johnston, D. (1995b). Child custody issues of women prisoners: A preliminary report from the CHICAS project. *The Prison Journal, 75*, 222–239.

Johnston, D. (1995c). Effects of parental incarceration. In K. Gabel & D. Johnston (Eds.), *Children of incarcerated parents* (pp. 59-88). New York: Lexington Books.

Johnston, D. (1995d). Intervention. In K. Gabel & D. Johnston (Eds.), *Children of incarcerated parents* (pp. 199–236). New York: Lexington Books.

The Osborne Association. (1993). How can I help? Working with children of incarcerated parents. In *Serving special children* (vol. 1). New York: The Osborne Association.

Sabrina N., In re. 60 Cal.App.4th 996, 1998 WL 7763 (Cal.App. 2 Dist.) (Jan. 1998).

Smith, B., & Elstein, S. G. (1994). *Children on hold: Improving the response to children whose parents are arrested and incarcerated.* Washington, DC: U.S. Department of Health and Human Services (report funded by the Children's Bureau).

Snell, T. (1994). *Women in prison*. Washington, DC: U.S. Department of Justice, Bureau of Justice Statistics (special report).

U.S. Department of Health and Human Services, Children's Bureau. (1997). *National study of protective, preventive and reunification services delivered to children and their families*. Washington, DC: U.S. Government Printing Office.

U.S. Department of Justice. (1997). *Correctional populations in the United States, 1995*. Washington, DC: U.S. Department of Justice, Bureau of Justice Statistics.

Virginia Commission on Youth. (1992). *Report to the Governor and the Virginia General Assembly on the study of the needs of children whose parents are incarcerated*.

Women's Prison Association. (1996). When a mother is arrested: How the criminal justice and child welfare systems can work together more effectively: A needs assessment initiated by the Maryland Department of Human Resources.

Supporting Families and Children of Mothers in Jail: An Integrated Child Welfare and Criminal Justice Strategy

1

Pamela Covington Katz

Charged with the responsibility for protecting children and preserving families, the child welfare system needs to pay special attention to women in jail and their families. Jails provide an opportunity to reach families early in the criminal justice process. This article explores why working with women in jail and their children is within the scope of the child welfare system's mandate; describes the pressures on the criminal justice and child welfare systems that prevent either from working effectively with these families; and suggests a collaborative strategy for working more effectively with mothers in jail and their children.

Pamela Covington Katz, J.D., is Consultant for Special Projects, Women's Prison Association, New York, NY.

On any one day, the 3,300 jails in the United States hold more than half a million people, including 59,296 women, at a cost of more than $9.6 billion to local governments [Gilliard & Beck 1998; Cornelius 1996]. Women are the fastest growing population in jail; their numbers have increased more than 300% since 1985, largely as a result of a dramatic increase in the number of women incarcerated for nonviolent drug or drug-related offenses [Beck & Gilliard 1997; Snell 1992]. Although the direct expenses of operating and constructing jails are staggering, they do not begin to reflect the costs to children, families, and communities of locking up an ever-increasing number of nonviolent drug offenders—particularly women who are often the sole caregivers for their children. In fact, mothers in jail typically leave behind two or more children [Snell 1992].

Administered by local governments, jails are the entry gate into the criminal justice system. Jails confine pretrial detainees (inmates who were arrested and are awaiting trial). Children and families are particularly at risk during this time because pretrial detainees do not know how long they are likely to be away from their children. With little help or even access to a telephone, jailed mothers must find caregivers to look after their children. These caregivers, in turn, often assume care for the children with few resources to handle their new responsibility. Meanwhile, the children's lives may be turned upside down as they are shuffled from home to home with little information about what has happened to their mothers.

In addition to holding pretrial detainees, jails confine women who have been convicted of minor crimes, typically misdemeanors, with sentences of less than one year. Often referred to as "sentenced" inmates, these individuals will not serve their sentences in prisons, which are run by state or federal governments and hold inmates convicted of felonies. Unfortunately, jails generally lack the rehabilitative programs often found in prisons, such as drug treatment, educational opportunities, and parenting classes. Although women sentenced to jail have committed less serious crimes than those in prisons, their lives are often marred by the same risk factors—including substance abuse and long histories of victimization—that can be so damaging to children and families. Without help, many of these women will be in and out of jail for a large portion of their children's lives.

Charged with responsibility for protecting children and preserving families, the child welfare system needs to pay special attention to women in jail and their families. Jails provide an opportunity to reach families early in the criminal justice process, when finding a stable home for the children is of critical concern. Jails can also provide an opening for an effective intervention with families whose children are already in out-of-home care or at serious risk of placement.

This article explores why working with women in jail and their children and families is within the scope of the child welfare system's mandate and describes the pressures on the criminal justice and child welfare systems that can prevent either system from working effectively with this population. It concludes by suggesting a collaborative strategy for working more effectively with mothers in jail and their children that can serve the interests of both systems.

Impact on the Child Welfare System

At a time when so many issues demand the attention of public administrators, when welfare reform threatens to leave many impoverished families unprotected, and when most public agencies have to do more with less, it can be disheartening to hear that there is yet another population that needs help. Most public agencies struggle to fulfill their narrowly defined mandates, without looking for more places to spend their already thinly stretched resources. Women in jail and their families, however, are not a "new" group in need of special help. These families already fall within the confines of the child welfare system's commitment to protecting children and preserving families: as discussed below, many of their children are already in out-of-home care and most of the rest are at risk of placement.

Not only are these children at increased risk of abuse and neglect, but the overwhelming evidence demonstrates that they often face numerous other challenges that put them at risk. Children of incarcerated mothers often display low self-esteem, anxiety, low achievement motivation, poor conscience development, poor social adjustment and peer relations, depression, juvenile delinquency, aggression, drug abuse, and other problems [Virginia Commission on Youth 1993]. Ultimately, one in ten will be incarcerated themselves by the time they reach adulthood [Johnston 1995b].

Children in Out-of-Home Care with Mothers Currently or Previously in Jail

On any given day, approximately 7% of the mothers currently in jail have children in out-of-home care [Snell 1992]. This statistic, however, vastly understates the number of children in care whose mothers have been in jail at some point in their lives, since these children often remain in out-of-home care longer than their mothers are in jail. With nearly a million women admitted to jails each year, the number of children in out-of-home care who are affected is undoubtedly much higher than available data suggest [Beck et al. 1995]. If the population of women in jail continues to increase at its current rate of 10% a year, an even larger number of children in out-of-home care will have mothers in jail in the future [Gilliard & Beck 1998].

Children of Mothers in Jail at Risk of Out-of-Home Placement

Three characteristics common to jailed women—substance abuse, long histories of victimization, and recurring criminal justice involvement—combine to put children at increased risk of abuse or neglect. The vast majority of women in jail are addicted to alcohol or other drugs. One study found that 61% of the women in a municipal jail used cocaine at least once a week prior to their arrest and 83% had significant problems related to drug use [Bussey et al. 1995]. These statistics are significant because substance abuse is linked with an increased rate of child abuse or neglect [Zuckerman 1994]. Thus, even without the additional problems created by arrest and incarceration, a mother's drug addiction can undermine her ability to provide consistent nurturing care to her children.

Further, women in jail often come from fragmented and abusive families and face continuing abuse as adults. More than 17% of the women in jail lived in a family foster home, agency, or institution while growing up [Snell 1992]. At least a third were raised by a parent or guardian who abused alcohol or drugs [Snell 1992]. Many—if not most—have suffered tremendous abuse, including both physical and sexual abuse, often beginning in childhood [Bussey et al. 1995; Johnston 1994; Snell 1992]. In fact, the high rate of alcohol and other drug addictions among women in jail may result from their repeated abuse, as many women may use drugs, in part, to self-medicate the painful feelings associated with these traumatic events [Zuckerman 1994].

If the mother's partner is currently abusing her, her children are likely to be exposed to that violence at home. Further, if the mother has not had the opportunity to deal with her own history of child abuse or to recognize the ways it might affect how she raises her children, it can impair her ability to nurture and provide for her own children [Davis 1990].

Women in jail and their families face not just the increased risk of abuse and neglect, often associated with childhood abuse, drug addiction, and domestic violence, but also the trauma and disorganization created by the mothers' crime, arrest, and incarceration [Johnston 1994]. One in five children will witness their mother's arrest [Johnston 1995a]. Further, such arrests typically lead to tremendous instability for children, who are often shuffled among homes and caregivers and separated from their siblings [Johnston 1995b]. Most children have little contact with their mothers while their mothers are in jail [Johnston 1995a].

A mother's release from jail rarely alleviates the problems for her family. After release from jail, women often have difficulty finding housing, drug and alcohol counseling, mental health counseling, employment, medical care, family support, or child care [Bussey et al. 1995]. Without these resources, many women are unable to lead crime-free, drug-free lives. Two-thirds of the women in jail have been previously convicted and almost half have been previously incarcerated in either prison or jail [Snell 1992]. Women's interactions with the criminal justice system often occur in a cycle that begins with accelerated drug use, followed by a drug-related crime, and arrest [Johnston 1994]. Upon release from jail, many women attempt to remain drug-free or at least reduce their drug needs [Johnston 1994]. As their reentry efforts fail, however, their drug use increases [Johnston 1994].

The Need for a Collaborative Strategy

Despite the apparent need to provide support to children and families of women in jail, pressures within the criminal justice and child welfare systems often prevent either system from working effectively with women in jail and their families. Typically, women in jail do not have a copy of the written child welfare case plan for their children [Beckerman 1994]. Further, women in jail often do not receive adequate notice of upcoming family court hearings or cannot get to court even if they receive notice [Beckerman 1994]. Many do not receive visits from their children and have little contact with their child welfare case workers [Beckerman 1994]. In addition, women in jail often receive few services (such as drug treatment) to address the underlying causes of crime, and little assistance in reintegrating themselves into their communities [Bussey et al. 1995].

Too Many Families in Need, Too Few Resources

Both the criminal justice and child welfare systems have seen large increases in the number of women and children they must serve. The number of abused or neglected children nearly doubled from

1986 to 1993 and the nature of their injuries has become increasingly serious [Broadhurst & Sedlak 1996]. These large increases in the number of abused or neglected children affect every aspect of the child welfare system. Child protective services cannot keep up with the dramatic rise in abuse or neglect reports [Broadhurst & Sedlak 1996]. Family foster care services have difficulty recruiting enough foster parents or providing them with the help they need to care for the children. Growing case worker caseloads make reunifying families or finding other permanent homes for children difficult.

Meanwhile, the number of jail inmates, both male and female, has nearly doubled in the last decade [Bureau of Justice Statistics 1997]. Increased populations put additional pressure on every aspect of jail management. Most inmates are in facilities with more than 500 inmates—and some have more than 2,000 [Beck et al. 1995]. In many jails, the physical conditions of the aging facilities exacerbate space constraints [Cornelius 1996]. Resources can barely provide the security staff necessary to maintain ever-increasing populations [Cornelius 1996]. Overcrowding makes jails difficult to manage, causes stress for inmates and staff, and decreases the jails' ability to explore family-friendly visiting policies or to offer programs, including drug treatment, that require both program staff and additional security staff [Beck & Gilliard 1997; Cornelius 1996]. Jails struggle to simply handle their mandated responsibilities—maintaining security, transporting pretrial detainees to and from court appearances, screening incoming inmates for infectious diseases, feeding inmates, and providing medical services to inmates who are often in poor health (6% of the jail population is HIV positive) [Beck & Gilliard 1997; Cornelius 1996].

Political Pressures

Political pressures create "one size fits all" policies that cannot be adapted to the needs of particular children and families. Strict guidelines on sentencing and restrictions on the length of time that children can remain in care undermine the criminal justice and child welfare systems' flexibility in responding to the particular needs of families. Mandatory sentencing for drug offenses results in more money being spent to lock women up for longer periods of time. Too often, these women are returned to their communities without efforts being made to adequately address the underlying drug addictions that led to their incarceration. Meanwhile, the federal Adoption and Safe Families Act of 1997 (P.L. 105–89) requires states to move to sever parental rights after the child has spent 15 of the most recent 22 months in out-of-home care. This rule creates a hardship for mothers in jail whose children are in out-of-home care. The mean sentence for women in jail is six months and women often leave jail unprepared to resume care for their children [Snell 1992]. Jails frequently do not provide the drug treatment or parenting classes most women must complete before they can reunify their families [Bussey et al. 1995; Wood 1982]. Further, upon release, women often have difficulty finding services such as housing, employment, or child care that would allow them to care for their children [Bussey et al. 1995].

Inadequate Cross-Systems Cooperation and Exchange of Information

Far from supporting each others' efforts in working with women in jail and their families, the criminal justice and child welfare systems often seem to be at odds with each other. The difficulties encountered in working with these families frustrate workers in both systems and create a sense of ill will toward both the family in need and the system perceived as originating the obstacle at hand [Women's Prison Association 1996a, 1996b]. In focus groups, child welfare professionals routinely describe how frustrating it can be to arrange visits or to contact a mother in jail [Women's Prison Association 1996a, 1996b]. Meanwhile, their criminal justice counterparts have difficulty accessing appropriate child welfare services for the family or contacting the child welfare case worker already assigned to work with the mother in jail and her children [Women's Prison Association 1996a, 1996b]. Faced with the magnitude of problems that typically confront these families, workers within each system can feel overwhelmed [Women's Prison Association 1996a, 1996b]. Finally, in the absence of a cross-systems exchange of information, families may receive duplicate or unnecessary interventions, such as drug screening or parenting training, while other needed services, such as discharge planning, are not provided [Women's Prison Association 1996a, 1996b].

Inadequate Facilities and Training

Women in jail are a relatively small fraction (11%) of the total jail population and their children are a small percentage of the total number of children in out-of-home care or at risk of abuse or neglect [Bureau of Justice Statistics 1997]. For the most part, jails are designed and administered to hold men, who are usually not the primary caregivers for their children before their arrest [Johnston 1995b]. Jails may not ask incoming inmates if they have made adequate arrangements for their children's care or even if they have children. Jail staff may not receive any training to address the family-related issues that can be pressing for women in jail, such as helping mothers to arrange for their children to be registered for school or to deal with the trauma they are experiencing. Meanwhile, because the children of women in jail are a relatively small and often hidden population of the total number of children in out-of-home care or at risk of placement, child welfare agencies may not provide training for case workers on how to work with these families, including how to arrange visits, what resources are available to support the family, and what requirements women have to fulfill as conditions of their release [Women's Prison Association 1996a, 1996b].

Lack of Assistance with Placement Decisions

Upon their arrest, women must, under pressure, make difficult placement decisions that will be pivotal in determining the quality of their children's care and whether the women will maintain a relationship with their children. Evaluating the best placement option involves difficult legal, psychological, social, and financial considerations. The mother's separation from her community and family undermines her ability to make a sound decision. Further, caregivers often assumes responsibility for children with little information about how long their mothers are likely to be away and with limited resources to address the traumas the children have experienced. Even if the mother was not living with her children before the arrest, her arrest and incarceration can still be traumatic for her children and their caregiver, and can disrupt family relationships. Prior to her arrest, the mother might have been seeing her children regularly and contributing to their care even if she was not the primary caregiver.

Difficulty Facilitating Contact between Jailed Mothers and Their Children

By their very nature, jails isolate people from their communities and their families. Visiting and telephone contact may seem deceptively simple to arrange, but in fact, any contact between inmates and people outside the facility poses serious security issues for the facility [Perez 1996]. The jail's security precautions must be geared to the occasional inmate who will try to sneak contraband into the facility, possibly even in her child's diaper [Perez 1996]. Jails, unlike prisons, almost universally require noncontact visits: mothers and their children must communicate over the phone through glass or a thick wire mesh [Perez 1996]. Thus, although jails are typically closer to the children's homes than prisons, visiting is often much less child-friendly. For this reason, some women in jail may not want their children to visit them [Henriques 1982]. Further, visiting hours may not coincide with the child welfare case worker's work day and arranging special visiting times is difficult [Women's Prison Association 1996a]. Both criminal justice and child welfare staff express reservations about whether children should visit their parents in jail, despite overwhelming evidence that visiting benefits both parent and child [Henriques 1982; Johnston 1995; Women's Prison Association 1996a]. Visiting is particularly important for the children of women in jail because it allows the children to see that their mothers are safe [Johnston 1995].

Jail facilities also severely limit inmate access to telephones. Local calls typically cost more than regular pay phones, and long-distance calls must be made "collect"—at a cost to the inmates' families that many cannot afford.

Turning Crisis into Opportunity: A Collaborative Strategy

At a cursory glance, the goals of the local criminal justice and child welfare systems might seem widely divergent. Yet as we have seen, both systems work with many of the same women and families. Although each system might define success differently, both provide (or refer women to) similar services, including drug treatment, parenting and life skills training, and educational programs. Ultimately, by successfully treating the mother's drug addiction and healing the fractured family, the criminal justice system will reduce recidivism rates and the child welfare system will preserve and reunify more families. Toward these ends, both systems have a common interest in (1) providing opportunities for mothers to plan for their children's care, to maintain and build relationships with their children, and to help their children to heal from the trauma they experience; and (2) encouraging mothers in jail to live sober lives and develop new skills that will enable them to cope with the pressures of living in their communities and raising their children.

Providing Opportunities for Mothers to Plan for and Help Their Children

By allowing mothers to actively participate in placement decisions and, to whatever extent possible, continue to exercise control over their children's care, the criminal justice and child welfare systems can reduce their anxiety, enhance reunification efforts, and ease the transition for the children. Women who participate in making the placement decision tend to be more satisfied with their children's living situation [Henriques 1982]. Reducing the mother's anxiety about her children's care helps jail administrators meet their short-term goal of managing and controlling inmate behavior [Perez 1996]. Further, children tend to cooperate more with plans for their care that their mothers developed in their behalf [Henriques 1982]. Mothers are often ardent advocates for their children and, possibly, in the best position to provide information about their needs. Finally, keeping mothers involved in their children's lives is critical to the success of any reunification efforts.

Jurisdictions can undertake any number of different steps to help women make appropriate placement decisions and to equip caregivers to look after the children. Jail counselors should receive training from the child welfare system on how to help women plan for their children's care and to advise women about their rights and responsibilities as parents. Closer communication and connection between the local jail counseling staff and the child welfare system could facilitate finding the child in the child welfare system or the mother in the jail system. A representative from the child welfare system could make weekly, bimonthly, or monthly visits to the local detention center to answer inmates' questions about their children's care.

Many services can be provided at low cost through volunteers. For example, the Incarcerated Mothers Law Project, a collaboration between the Women's Prison Association and the Volunteers of Legal Service, relies on volunteer attorneys to provide women in the New York City jail system with access to legal counseling. Community-based family preservation or support efforts could reach out to caregivers looking after children of mothers in jail. Information on the criminal justice process, visiting, and how to get help in caring for one's children could be disseminated at the criminal court, through the public defender's office, at community centers, and so forth.

An important part of helping children cope with the trauma

they have experienced is establishing regular visiting for them with their mothers, beginning as soon after the arrest as possible [Johnston 1995a]. Visiting allows children to discuss their emotional reactions to the separation, parents to work out feelings of separation and loss and to be better able to help children with these issues, and both parents and children to see each other realistically [Johnston 1995a]. Several programs across the country demonstrate that it is possible to safely allow contact visits in a jail setting. For example, in Bexar County, Texas, inmates who participate in the MATCH/PATCH Programs can receive weekly contact visits with their children. Children ages newborn to 16 years old visit in a child-friendly environment, stocked with toys, books, area rugs, children's furniture, a rocking chair, and even a crib, which are contributed by businesses. After visits, inmate parents and their children meet in separate groups to discuss their visiting experiences. Far from creating security problems, the program has improved inmate behavior, decreased property damage, lessened the potential for injuries to officers and inmates, and decreased disciplinary problems [Perez 1996].

Short of creating an entirely new visiting program, it is possible to improve visiting conditions. For example, one facility in Maryland was willing to explore allowing child welfare case workers to use the booths reserved for lawyers for children's visits [Women's Prison Association 1996a]. Although these booths permitted only noncontact visiting, they provided the children with privacy, and allowed them to sit down and to see their parent [Women's Prison Association 1996a]. The normal visiting area was a row of 6" by 12" narrow windows about 5 feet off the ground, with only little dividers separating each window [Women's Prison Association 1996a].

Further, the child welfare system might negotiate for special passes that allow case workers to bypass the regular visiting routine. The jail might be willing to set up special visiting days or places for children in out-of-home care. As jurisdictions make plans to build new facilities, the advocacy of the child welfare system might make the difference between contact visiting in a child-friendly room and noncontact visiting. The child welfare system could also provide training for case workers or foster parents on how to handle visits to correctional facilities and issue clear guidelines on the appropriateness of these visits. Finally, jail facilities could routinely update local child welfare agencies on any changes in their visiting policies.

Encouraging Mothers in Jail to Live Sober Lives and Develop New Skills

Clearly, a parent's arrest is a family crisis. But in many ways, it can also be a beginning, a unique opportunity for an effective intervention. Frequently, incarcerated women find themselves sober for the first time in a long time. They begin to see more clearly the consequences of their actions. It is at this moment that many are sincerely committed to reclaiming their lives. An important part of this healing involves creating strong relationships with their children.

To succeed, work with mothers in jail requires a high level of collaboration between the criminal justice and child welfare system to link services inside the jail with those in the community and to respond comprehensively to the families' needs. While in jail, many women can be engaged in participating in drug treatment and other programs. To be effective, however, treatment must continue after the woman's release [Anglin et al. 1994]. Further, it must be combined with family services that help women care for their children [Anglin et al. 1994]. Finally, for many women—particularly drug offenders—devising community-based sanctions that allow the women to address their alcohol or other drug addiction while continuing to care for their children may be the most appropriate course of action [Chesney-Lind & Immarigeon 1992].

Collaboration in service provision should occur at the policy, program, and practice levels. Jurisdictions could explore community-based alternatives to incarceration that allow women to live in the community with their children while they seek drug treatment. In these programs, criminal justice monitoring can ensure compliance with court-ordered drug treatment while child welfare services can help the mothers improve their parenting skills, care for their children, and ensure that the children get the help they need. For example, although rapid turnover makes programming in jails difficult, the Baltimore Women's Awareness and Acupuncture Center has demonstrated that it is possible to provide drug treatment in a jail setting. Its program addresses drug dependency by using acupuncture, individual and group counseling, group education, and AA/NA in a two-week cycle, and emphasizes community-based aftercare and continuity of treatment after release [Women's Prison Association 1996a].

Short of starting new programs, there is still much that the child welfare and criminal justice systems can do to work together effectively. Links between the jail's counseling and program staff and the child welfare agency's case workers can provide continuity of treatment. Joint discharge planning can ensure that women succeed once they are released. Once a parent is released, the child welfare case worker can coordinate a case conference with the parent, the children's caregiver, the parent's probation officer, the drug treatment counselor, and other professionals working with the family to sketch out a plan for the family.

Conclusion

Generating better outcomes for children of women in jail will ultimately require nothing less than providing effective drug and alcohol treatment for women in jail, helping children deal with the trauma they have experienced, understanding more about how parental incarceration affects children and the intergenerational cycle of criminal justice involvement, creating continuous support for women as they return to their communities, and, ideally, providing community-based alternatives to incarceration. This is a huge undertaking that will require the combined resources and expertise of many government systems, especially the criminal justice and child welfare systems. Nonetheless, if criminal justice and child welfare systems start small by identifying their shared commitments and taking actions consistent with those commitments, together they can yield better outcomes for women in jail, their children, and their families. ◆

References

Anglin, M. D., Prendergast, M. L., & Wellisch, J. (1994). *Drug abusing women offenders: Results of a national survey.* Washington, DC: National Institute of Justice.

Beck, A. J., Perkins, C. A., & Stephan, J. J. (1995). *Bureau of Justice Statistics bulletin: Jails and jail inmates 1993–94.* Washington, DC: U.S. Department of Justice, Bureau of Justice Statistics.

Beckerman, A. (1994). Mothers in prison: Meeting the prerequisite conditions for permanency planning. *Social Work, 39,* 9–13.

Broadhurst, D. D., & Sedlak, A. J. (1996). *Executive summary of the third national incidence study of child abuse and neglect.* Washington, DC: U.S. Department of Health and Human Services.

Bussey, J., Lunghofer, L., Singer, M. I., & Song, L. (1995). The psychosocial issues of women serving time in jail. *Social Work, 40,* 103–112.

Chesney-Lind, M., & Immarigeon, R. (1992). *Women's prisons: Overcrowded and overused.* San Francisco: National Council on Crime and Delinquency.

Cornelius, G. F. (1996). *Jails in America: An overview of issues (2nd ed.).* Lanham, MD: American Correctional Association.

Davis, S. K. (1990). Chemical dependency in women: A description of its effects and outcome on adequate parenting. *Journal of Substance Abuse Treatment, 7,* 225–232.

Gilliard, D. K., & Beck, A. J. (1998). *Bureau of Justice Statistics bulletin: Prison and jail inmates at midyear 1997.* Washington, DC: U.S. Department of Justice, Bureau of Justice Statistics.

Henriques, Z. W. (1982). *Imprisoned mothers and their children: A descriptive and analytical study.* Washington, DC: University Press of America.

Johnston, D. (1994). *Report number 8: The jailed mothers study.* Pasadena, CA: Pacific Oaks College and Children's Programs.

Johnston, D. (1995). *Report number 16: Jail visiting environments.* Pasadena, CA: Pacific Oaks College and Children's Programs.

Johnston, D. (1996). Effects of parental incarceration. In K. Gabel & D. Johnston (Eds.), *Children of incarcerated parents* (pp. 59–88). Boston, MA: Lexington Books.

Perez, J. A. (1996, November/December). Inmate parenting contact visitation programs: Why implement them? *American Jails, 10*(5), 31–36.

Snell, T. L. (1992). *Bureau of Justice Statistics special report: Women in jail 1989.* Washington, DC: U.S. Department of Justice, Bureau of Justice Statistics.

Virginia Commission on Youth. (1993). *House document no. 32: Report of the Virginia Commission on Youth on the study of the needs of children whose parents are incarcerated.* Richmond, VA: Virginia Commission on Youth.

Women's Prison Association. (1996a). *When a mother is arrested: How the criminal justice and child welfare systems can work together more effectively.* Baltimore: Maryland Department of Human Resources.

Women's Prison Association. (1996b). *Bridging the gap between the child welfare and criminal justice systems in New York City.* New York: Women's Prison Association.

Wood, D. (1982). *Women in jail.* Milwaukee, WI: The Benedict Center for Criminal Justice.

Zuckerman, B. (1994). Effects on parents and children. In D. J. Besharov (Ed.), *When drug addicts have children: Reorienting child welfare's response* (pp. 49–61). Washington, DC: Child Welfare League of America.

Charting a Course: Meeting the Challenge of Permanency Planning for Children with Incarcerated Mothers

2

Adela Beckerman

Case workers involved in permanency planning for children whose mothers are incarcerated must assess the family's strengths, the mother's capacity to assume parental responsibilities, and the integrity of the parent-child relationship; and address concerns regarding the short- and long-term effects of the children's socioemotional dislocation and the merits of their retaining a relationship with their mothers. At the same time, correctional policies and practices delineate the nature and extent of contacts with the mother and the mother's access to rehabilitative programs. Agency guidelines, practice tools, and advocacy initiatives must be developed to help practitioners meet these challenges. An initial review of the Adoption and Safe Families Act suggests the need for close monitoring of the impact of its mandates to shorten the time for moving children toward permanency and its weakening of the expectation for "reasonable efforts" to be made to reunify families.

Adela Beckerman, Ph.D., ACSW, is Program Professor of Research and Evaluation, Fischer Center for the Advancement of Education, Nova Southeastern University, North Miami Beach, FL.

C ase workers developing permanency plans for children in out-of-home care must assess the integrity of the children's relationships with their parents and the feasibility of family reunification, and implement plans that promise permanence through reunification, adoption, or alternative living arrangements. When a mother is incarcerated, the process of developing and implementing permanency plans presents contours and characteristics that differ from those typically encountered. Until recently, case workers did not often work with children in care whose mothers were incarcerated; the number of incarcerated women in the U.S. was small. In the past 25 years, however, the number of women in state and federal prisons increased from about 6,000 to 74,730, and the average daily population of female inmates in local jails rose from 19,077 to 59,296 between 1985 and 1997 [Gilliard & Beck 1998; Mumola & Beck 1997]. More than 75% of incarcerated women are mothers, the majority of whom had custody of dependent children prior to their incarceration [Bloom & Steinhart 1993; Greenfeld & Minor-Harper 1991; Snell 1994]. While most of their children are cared for by grandmothers, other relatives, and friends, as many as 13% are in out-of-home care [Bloom & Steinhart 1993; Festler 1991; McGowan & Blumenthal 1978; Snell 1994; Stanton 1980].

This article addresses the challenges facing case workers who manage cases in which the mother is incarcerated, and discusses the need for child welfare agencies to develop practice guidelines and resources in anticipation of such cases. The passage of the Adoption and Safe Families Act (P.L. 105-89) in late 1997 creates a sense of urgency for such development. The Act's expectations will likely accentuate the difficulties that already present themselves when managing cases involving incarcerated parents.

Assessing the Mother's Capabilities

Constraints on an incarcerated mother's ability to plan and prepare for her postrelease life have long presented formidable challenges for case planning. The ease with which a prognosis for the mother's rehabilitation or reunification with her children can be developed is restricted by the limited availability of discharge planning, counseling, substance abuse treatment, vocational or parent education, and similar services for women in jails and prisons [Gray et al. 1995; Schoenbauer 1986]. Such services are needed because the majority of incarcerated mothers have a history of family and personal problems [Adalist-Estrin 1994; Owen & Bloom 1995]. In the absence of meaningful support and rehabilitation services, the mother's ability to alter her life course and successfully reunify and sustain her family as a healthy, viable unit is severely hampered. The incarcerated mother may be pressured to make use of the narrow range of inadequate services available and to "test out" any newly acquired skills in the artificial setting of the jail or prison [Beckerman & Hutchison 1988].

Constraints on the case worker's ability to maintain contact with the mother, whether in the form of visits, telephone calls, or correspondence, are also troublesome. Contact is central to the assessment process and is a prerequisite if the mother is to be involved in permanency planning and the case worker is to monitor adherence to plans. Correctional policies and practices, however, delineate and limit the nature and extent of possible contacts. Typically, inmates cannot receive incoming calls and must place outgoing calls collect. Specific procedures must be followed if correspondence is to be sent or received. Visits are similarly regulated: hours are limited and exacting procedures must be followed prior to and during visits. In addition, prisons for women are usually located at a considerable distance from their home communities. Extensive time and money are spent when case workers visit [Beckerman 1989; Hairston & Hess 1988]. Beckerman [1994] found that contact by the case worker may be limited. Almost half of the imprisoned mothers she surveyed received little or no correspondence from their case workers, two-thirds did not receive a copy of the case plan, and one-third were not notified of court hearings reviewing the status of those plans.

Other factors also inhibit contact between the mother and the case worker as well as between the mother and her children. For example, in the confusion that ensues when a mother is initially arrested and confined, it may be difficult for her to find out whether her children have been placed, the location of their family foster home, or the name of their case worker [Bloom & Steinhart 1993]. To camouflage her embarrassment, shame, and feelings that she does not deserve to have contact with her children, the mother may trivialize or subvert efforts intended to enhance reunification. She may feign disinterest or disregard, or be reluctant to have her children know she is in prison and to have them visit [Hairston 1991].

Central to permanency planning is the need to assess the merits and feasibility of reunification and fashion a permanency plan. The mother's ability and willingness to assume parental responsibilities need to be closely reviewed and an assessment made of her capacity to provide emotionally, developmentally, and physically for her children. Efforts by the mother to maintain regular contact with her children and their case worker, participate in programs, and attend court hearings are perceived as a demonstration of cooperation, investment, and commitment. An examination of the integrity of the mother's relationship with her children both prior to and during her incarceration is appropriate. Hairston [1991] argues that despite the dysfunctional aspects of a mother's preincarceration life, one cannot assume that she has abdicated her parental responsibilities or wishes to do so. Hairston found that the majority of mothers had primary responsibility for their children and were intimately involved in raising them. A comprehensive assessment is called for that takes these factors and the child's "best interests" into consideration.

P.L. 105-89 shortens the timeline within which assessment and establishment of a permanency plan can be accomplished and forces the initiation of termination proceedings in specified cases. Most states consider the inability to care for one's children for a prolonged period of time or a record of nonperformance of expected duties—such as the absence of contact with one's children—as evidence of abandonment and grounds for termination of parental rights [Amadio & Mulryan 1992; Beckerman 1991; Brooks & Bahna 1994; Genty 1991; Hairston 1991]. The Adoption and Safe Families Act mandates that a permanency plan be in place 12 months after a child's placement, rather than the 18 months called for in previous legislation. At the same time, the expectation that "reasonable efforts" be made to facilitate reunification is excused if a court has found that there are "aggravated circumstances" such as abandonment. Given the cumbersome aspects of maintaining contact with the mother, determining the date when a mother will be released from prison, assuring that the necessary rehabilitation and discharge planning will have occurred, and developing documentation of what is in a child's "best interests," formulation of a convincing plan for reunification becomes increasingly difficult and or even impossible.

Impact of Parental Incarceration on Children

As part of the permanency planning process, the socioemotional impact of the mother's incarceration and the resulting experiences that confront her children need to be examined. The merits of seeking reunification or other alternatives need to be assessed and a permanency plan developed that delineates a cohort of recommended interventions that are in the "best interests" of the child. Children need to be consulted about the goals of their permanency plans—regardless of whether those plans call for adoption, reunification, or another alternative. While the modality and rigor of the children's input will vary with their age and developmental level, they can be empowered by being given a meaningful role in permanency planning and being kept abreast of and involved in the decisionmaking process.

Often children feel somehow responsible for their mother's incarceration or cultivate what may be unrealistic fantasies of what their family life will be like when their mother is released [Stanton

1980]. Their reactions are influenced by their relationship with their parent and their developmental stage [Johnston 1995a]. Children are aware of the stigma associated with their mother's criminal activities and her imprisonment, and experience embarrassment and anger [Hannon et al. 1984]. A "conspiracy of silence" sometimes surfaces in which children and their caregivers do not discuss where the mother is, her criminal behavior, or her future return to the community [Kampfner 1995]. Unspoken questions linger about whether the children will follow in their parents' footsteps. Several studies have noted the presence of behavioral, learning, and social difficulties [Baunach 1985; Bloom & Steinhart 1993; Stanton 1980]. Kampfner [1995] observed and interviewed children who were visiting their mothers in prison and found evidence that they experience depression and sleeping problems, and have flashbacks to traumatic experiences related to their mother's arrest. Children's reactions to their mother's incarceration are, however, influenced by confounding variables. Much of the behavioral, emotional, and learning difficulties children display is likely related to the history of continuous or sporadic disruptions that preceded the mother's incarceration [Johnston 1995a, 1995b]. A fuller understanding of the interplay of the constellation of experiences that impact children before and during their mother's incarceration is needed to guide permanency planning policies and practices.

Studies of children in out-of-home care have repeatedly found a significant relationship between parent-child visits and the likelihood of reunification [Davis et al. 1996; Hess 1987; Oysterman & Benbenishty 1992]. Visits can provide opportunities for an incarcerated mother to offer support and to assure her children that she has not abandoned or rejected them. They can serve as a form of reality testing, providing exposure to the mother's living conditions (which are likely to be better than those envisioned by the child) [Johnston 1995b]. Despite this, the majority of mothers in jails and prisons receive few, if any, visits [Bloom & Steinhart

1993], primarily due to the cost and inconvenience associated with distance; most of the children live more than 100 miles from where their mothers are incarcerated. Additionally, caregivers may be reluctant to let the children visit.

Counseling and support services need to be incorporated into case plans to assist children with the impact of their mother's incarceration on their lives. Children need to be prepared for the contact they have with their mothers. Their mothers may act or look different than the children recall and the settings in which visits occur may afford little privacy or opportunity for physical contact. Even those children who welcome visits with their parents have been found to react with misbehavior and hostility [Baunach 1985; Walker 1983]. These reactions and behaviors are similar to those seen among children visiting a parent from whom they have been separated for other reasons such as parental divorce, extended hospitalization, or prolonged military service. Children and mothers need to be coached and counseled about the appropriate ways to interact during visits, on the telephone, and through correspondence, and about the feelings and reactions they have in anticipation of and after such contacts.

The impact of incarceration on all members of the mother's family needs to be reviewed and responded to. During incarceration, the structure of the family system and the relationships among its members shift. The incarcerated mother and the members of her family "are involved in separate struggles that require major adjustments. While prisoners struggle with both their inside and outside lives, the family is attempting to... include and exclude the prisoner" [Hannon et al. 1984: 255]. As a result, the placement of children in kinship care or attempts to obtain other forms of support from family members may resonate with the relatives' anger about the mother's criminal activities and imprisonment, and irritation about the demands being made. Relatives who are caregivers may also develop strong bonds with the children and resist the mother's re-entrance [Beckerman 1989].

Constructing Supports for Case Workers

Case workers must be able to determine what is in each child's "best interests," assess the strengths and capabilities of each mother, and develop and monitor plans that move each child into a home that promises permanence. Myriad considerations are presented in cases involving an incarcerated mother. Will a mother have the marketable vocational skills, parenting skills, and other assets and supports needed to successfully assume parental responsibilities? Will the mother's sentence exceed the statutory deadlines for moving her children out of care? Will the nature of the mother's crime prevent deliberations of reunification? What effect will P.L. 105-89's mandates of an abbreviated permanency planning timeline have? Case workers have little preparation for the parameters of and obstacles present in such cases. Mathias [1994] found that most case workers in one large private agency felt ill-prepared for the challenges. Having received no orientation or training, and little assistance with meeting the expectations of permanency planning in such cases, they had independently developed strategies.

Practice Guidelines and Resources

Clearly, diligent inquiry and assessment are needed to avoid faulty decisions and actions. Such efforts are time consuming and taxing for most case workers, who already manage large caseloads. Child welfare agencies must provide practice guidelines and resources to address the vagaries present in such cases. Instituting protocols that support case worker efforts to address the situations and dilemmas encountered can facilitate the effective and efficient use of case worker time and help maximize the quality of permanency planning services. An openness to reviewing current practices is needed. Several suggestions are offered, in part to initiate a dialogue about possible revisions and additions to existing service delivery systems. These include the development of case management handbooks and model case plans, the use of specially trained case workers dedicated to cases involving incarcerated parents, and involvement in advocacy initiatives.

Case Management Handbooks

Agencies should develop case management handbooks for use as an introduction and orientation to working with children whose parents are incarcerated, and as an ongoing reference. Relevant subjects such as the conditions under which termination of parental rights, physical reunification, or other alternatives should be sought should be included. In light of the standards articulated in P.L. 105-89, the handbook should provide guidance about when it is in a child's "best interests" to circumvent and preempt termination proceedings, and instructions about how and when this should be documented in case plans. In addition, guidelines should be included for cases where physical reunification is not feasible, yet it is in the child's "best interests" to maintain a relationship with his or her mother. Alternatives that do not completely foreclose the continuation of the parent-child relationship, such as open adoption or legal guardianship, need to be described [Allen 1992; Warsh et al. 1994], as well as provisions for visits, correspondence, and telephone contact.

The handbook should include a discussion of the impact of incarceration on all family members and suggest intervention methods that are congruent with the diverse cultural backgrounds and family systems of incarcerated women. Agency policies regarding maintaining communication with parents, expectations about the frequency of visits and other forms of contact, and timelines for permanency planning activities should be noted. Forms and instruments to be used for assessments and for recording plans and activities can be included, as well as sample letters to be used for maintaining contact with the mother and notifying her of upcoming court reviews.

Information about the different types of criminal offenses women commit and the factors that affect the length of their sentences should be present in the handbook. Provision for inclusion of a directory detailing the types of rehabilitation, vocational, and support programs in correctional facilities, including self-help groups such as Alcoholics Anonymous and battered women's groups, should be made. This could be accompanied by a description of the criteria for participation, the duration of each program, and a person to contact for more information. Correctional department regulations and procedures, such as those governing contact and the mother's ability to attend court hearings, should be described, and guidelines provided for preferable ways to follow these. To preempt common obstacles to effective permanency planning encountered by case workers in one large private agency, Mathias [1994] offered suggestions and guidelines in the form of a "self-instructional tool." They address how a case worker might prepare for a broad range of activities such as meetings with the mother and bringing children to a prison for visits. Such items can be readily incorporated into an agency's handbook.

Model Case Plans

Workers would likely find useful the compilation of a series of case plans that have been used in actual cases and found to be effective. Serving as models, each plan would offer a different configuration of circumstances and risk assessment factors. Goals would vary, targeting family reunification, termination of parental rights, and other alternatives. The models could offer recommendations in light of the children's chronological and developmental stage, as well as the history of the children's relationship with their mothers and the relative benefits of reunification or other alternatives, and articulate details of the responsibilities of each party, accompanied by a timeline and outcome measures. For example, mothers might be expected to participate in educational, rehabilitation and support programs, and regularly correspond with and telephone their children and case workers. Model plans would be mindful of the limitations presented by correctional regulations and suggest intervention services for the children as well.

The model plans would vary in their content and intent, but should be designed to cover the widest possible range of scenarios that a case worker might encounter. Thus, several of the model plans should reflect cases in which case workers have determined that it is in the child's "best interests" to prevent termination of parental rights and should appropriately document this in preparation for court hearings. In addition, several plans should incorporate a re-entry component, providing for a postrelease transition period during which the mother would establish a home for her children, refine her parenting skills, and become involved in community-based treatment and employment activities. Other plans could be directed toward terminating parental rights and moving the children into adoptive homes, incorporating provisions for continuation of the mother-child relationships (if advisable), and assisting children as they make the transition to their new status.

Specialized Case Workers

Agencies should give serious consideration to assigning case workers dedicated to managing cases in which a parent is incarcerated. These specialized case workers would develop a mastery of the criteria that guide decisions about reunification and termination of parental rights contained in state and federal law. They would develop competence in the varied areas of permanency planning with this client population, expertise in designing plans for mother-child contacts that are developmentally appropriate and emotionally beneficial for the children involved, and proficiency in the use of the assessment and planning tools most suited for these cases. Specialized case workers could culti-

vate relationships with correctional department staff who over-
see relevant operations and establish mechanisms that allow for
a smooth flow of information between the agency and correctional staff. Clearly, the handbooks and model case plans noted
above would be valuable resources.

Initiatives in support of the work of specialized case workers
would enhance the efficacy of their case management efforts. For
example, the agency could train a cadre of paid or volunteer es-
corts to assume responsibility for bringing children to jails and
prisons for visits, and conduct training for foster parents to stimulate partnerships in efforts to develop resiliency among children
in their care. The quality and stability of placements, especially
kinship care placements, necessitate addressing the attitudes and
feelings caregivers may have about the incarcerated mother, the
resistance they may articulate or demonstrate toward mother-
child contacts, and the fact that they have limited resources with
which to sustain the child in their home. Relationships could also
be established with programs in the community or in correctional
facilities that offer counseling, support groups, and other intervention services for the children of incarcerated parents (e.g.,
Prison MATCH [Mothers, Fathers and their Children] in
Pleasanton, California; PACT [Parents and Children Together] in
Fort Worth, Texas).

Advocacy

Agencies need to engage themselves in advocacy efforts directed
toward improving the range and quality of permanency planning services available to incarcerated women and their children
and assuring that case workers are effective in their efforts to
develop and implement permanency plans that are best for all
parties involved. Of great import is the need to monitor the interpretation and implementation of P.L. 105-89. The Act promises to
exaggerate rather than eradicate the obstacles to effective permanency planning that have long been evident. Areas found to be

problematic for effective practice need to be documented and advocacy campaigns initiated to modify or revise the legislation or its interpretation as needed.

Advocacy is also needed concerning the hours and conditions in which visits occur. Often visiting hours are incompatible with children's school schedules and the physical settings for visits are not conducive to the kind of dialogue and play children need to engage in with their mothers. Existing visiting programs in prisons and jails nationwide can be evaluated as part of an advocacy effort to develop a visiting program best suited for the needs of children and their families [Adalist-Estrin 1994].

Another serious obstacle that surfaces is the limited understanding that incarcerated mothers have of the permanency planning process. Advocacy efforts can call for the introduction of informational classes in all correctional facilities. Such classes are already in place in numerous facilities around the country. Their curricula include the clarification of statutory regulations and the grounds for abandonment and termination, and the importance of maintaining contact with the case worker and one's children and participating in case review hearings.

Attention also needs to be given to advocating for alternatives to incarceration. Community-based alternative programs may be warranted for the majority of women who are incarcerated for nonviolent offenses. Such settings—and the programming they offer—may be more conducive to permanency planning and to facilitating and sustaining family reunification.

Discussion and Conclusion

The precipitous rise in the number of women being confined in jails and prisons suggests that case workers are being called with increasing frequency to work with children in out-of-home care whose mothers are incarcerated and to address the obstacles to permanency that punctuate such cases. A review of the manner in which such cases are managed and the ways in which this might be improved is warranted. Possible approaches involve the development of handbooks, model case plans, the designation of specialized case workers, and agency advocacy.

To date, the child welfare community has responded in a rather ad-hoc manner to the issues that surface in out-of-home care cases in which a mother is incarcerated. This is reflected in the limited research available to inform permanency planning efforts. While studies have looked at the experiences of children in care in general [Barth 1997; Courtney 1995; Kufeldt et al. 1995], little information is available about the subset of children with incarcerated parents. Much of the research available is anecdotal or focuses on adult reports of children's feelings and behavior and does not control for the effect of intervening variables. A plethora of unanswered questions lingers: Does the experience of this subset of children differ from the population of children in care at large? How should such differences be reflected in permanency plans? What is the impact of a mother's incarceration on children? How does the impact vary with the children's age, developmental level, the extent of dislocation experienced, the mother's criminal history, and the children's prior living arrangements? Which types of assessment tools and instruments are most appropriate? Which interventions have been found to be effective? What factors predict successful case outcomes? When are the benefits of mother-child contacts significantly diminished by the behavior of the child or mother, or by the context within which they occur? What is the impact of P.L. 105-89 on the families of incarcerated mothers and on case workers? How can the strengths of the family unit and the child's "best interests" be measured and evaluated? What documentation is needed if a case worker determines that it is not in a child's "best interests" to terminate his or her parent's rights?

Research is needed to inform deliberations and decisionmaking. Cases involving an incarcerated parent introduce unique factors: the length of the sentence, the setting within which contact occurs, and the constraints on the mother to fully use educational and rehabilitative services. At the same time, monitoring is called for of the impact of the Adoption and Safe Families Act (P.L. 105-89) on permanency planning activities, the responsibilities of case workers, and the feasibility of planning for family reunification in cases involving incarcerated parents. ◆

References

Adalist-Estrin, A. (1994). Family support and criminal justice. In S. L. Kagan & B. Weissbourd (Eds.), *Putting families first* (pp. 161–185). San Francisco: Jossey Bass.

Allen, M. (1992). *Redefining family reunification*. Iowa City, IA: National Resource Center on Family Based Services.

Amadio, C. M., & Mulryan, R. (1992). Terminating parents rights of incarcerated parents. *Chicago Bar Association Record, 6,* 22–25.

Barth, R. P. (1997). Permanent placements for young children placed in foster care. *Children and Youth Services Review, 19,* 615–623.

Baunach, P. J. (1985). *Mothers in prison*. New Brunswick, NJ: Transaction Books.

Beckerman, A., & Hutchison, E. (1988). Direct practice approaches with offender-clients. In Rosenblatt, A. (Ed.), *For their own good?* (pp. 69–92). Albany, NY: State University of New York, Rockefeller Institute of Government.

Beckerman, A. (1991). Women in prison: The conflict between confinement and parental rights. *Social Justice, 18,* 171–183.

Beckerman, A. (1989). Incarcerated mothers and their children in foster care. *Children and Youth Services Review, 11,* 175–183.

Beckerman, A. (1994). Mothers in prison: Meeting the prerequisite conditions for permanency planning. *Social Work, 39,* 9–14.

Bloom, B., & Steinhart, D. (1993). *Why punish the children? A reappraisal of the children of incarcerated mothers in America.* San Francisco: National Council on Crime and Delinquency.

Brooks, J., & Bahna, K. (1994). "It's a Family Affair"—The incarceration of the American family: Confronting legal and social issues. *University of San Francisco Law Review, 28,* 271.

Courtney, M. E. (1995). Reentry to foster care of children returned to their families. *Social Service Review, 69,* 226–235.

Davis, I. P., Landsverk, J., Newton, R., & Ganger, W. (1996). Parenting, visiting and foster care reunification. *Children and Youth Services Review, 18,* 363–382.

Festler, S. (1991). *Mothers in the correctional system: Separation from children and reunification after incarceration* (unpublished doctoral dissertation, State University of New York at Albany).

Genty, P. M. (1991). Procedural due process rights of incarcerated parents in termination of parental rights proceedings: A fifty-state analysis. *Journal of Family Law, 30,* 757–846.

Gilliard, D. K. (1992, May). *Prisoners in 1992.* Washington, DC: U.S. Department of Justice, Bureau of Justice Statistics.

Gilliard, D. K., & Beck, A. J. (1998). *Prison and jail inmates at midyear 1997.* Washington, DC: U.S. Department of Justice, Bureau of Justice Statistics.

Gray, T., Mays, G. L., & Stohr, M. K. (1995). Inmate needs and programming in exclusively women's jails. *Prison Journal, 75,* 186–202.

Greenfeld, L. A., & Minor-Harper, S. (1991, March). *Women in prison.* Washington, DC: U.S. Department of Justice, Bureau of Justice Statistics.

Hairston, C. F. (1991). Mothers in jail: Parent-child separation and jail visitation. *Affilia, 6,* 9–27.

Hairston, C. F., & Hess, P. (1988, April). *Regulating parent-child communication in correctional settings.* Paper presented at the First National Conference on the Family and Corrections, Sacramento, CA.

Hannon, G., Martin, D., & Martin, M. (1984). Incarceration in the family: Adjustment of change. *Family Therapy, 11,* 253–260.

Hess, P. M. (1987). Parental visiting of children in foster care. *Children and Youth Services Review, 9,* 29–50.

Johnston, D. (1995a). Effects of parental incarceration. In K. Gabel & D. Johnston (Eds.), *Children of incarcerated parents* (pp. 59–88). New York: Lexington Books.

Johnston, D. (1995b). Parent-child visitation in the jail or prison. In K. Gabel & D. Johnston (Eds.), *Children of incarcerated parents* (pp. 135–143). New York: Lexington Books.

Kampfner, C. J. (1995). Post-traumatic stress reactions. In K. Gabel & D. Johnston (Eds.), *Children of incarcerated parents* (pp. 89–100). New York: Lexington Books.

Kufeldt, K., Armstrong, J., & Dorosh, M. (1995). How children in care view their own and their foster families: A research study. *Child Welfare, 74,* 695–716.

Mathias, S. (1994). *Development of a working model for a private foster care agency to facilitate planning considerations associated with archetypal cases involving an incarcerated parent* (unpublished practicum report, Nova Southeastern University, Fort Lauderdale, Florida).

McGowan, B. G., & Blumenthal, K. L. (1978). *Why punish the children?* Hackensack, NJ: National Council on Crime and Delinquency.

Mumola, C. J., & Beck, A. J. (June 1997). *Prisoners in 1996.* Washington, DC: U.S. Department of Justice, Bureau of Justice Statistics.

Owen, B., & Bloom, B. (1995). Profiling women prisoners. *Prison Journal, 75,* 165–187.

Oysterman, D., & Benbenishty, R. (1992). Keeping in touch: Ecological factors related to foster care visitation. *Child and Adolescent Social Work Journal, 9,* 541–554.

Schoenbauer, L. J. (1986). Incarcerated parents and their children—Forgotten families. *Law and Inequality, 4,* 579–601.

Snell, T. L. (1994). *Special report: Women in prison (NCJ–145321).* Washington, DC: U.S. Department of Justice, Bureau of Justice Statistics.

Stanton, S. (1980). *When mothers go to jail.* Lexington, MA: D.C. Heath.

Walker, N. (1983). Side-effects of incarceration. *British Journal of Criminology, 23,* 61–71.

Warsh, R., Maluccio, A., & Pine, B. (1994) *Teaching family reunification: A sourcebook.* Washington, DC: Child Welfare League of America.

In Whose Best Interest? The Impact of Changing Public Policy on Relatives Caring for Children with Incarcerated Parents

3

Susan Phillips and Barbara Bloom

Changes in criminal justice policy have resulted in the incarceration of an unprecedented number of parents. Consequently, more children than ever before are living with grandparents and other relatives while their parents are imprisoned. Historically, child welfare and criminal justice policy have been treated as distinct and unrelated areas of policy. This article discusses the interdependence of criminal justice policy, welfare reform legislation, and kinship foster care, and the impact of this interdependence on children whose parents are in jail or in prison.

Susan Phillips, LMSW, is Community Resource Development Coordinator, Parenting from Prison Program, Centers for Youth and Families, Little Rock, AR. Barbara Bloom, Ph.D., is Assistant Professor, Administration of Justice Department, San Jose State University, and Criminal Justice Consultant, Petaluma, CA.

The war on drugs and other criminal justice policies intended to get tough on crime have dramatically increased the number of people serving time in the United States. Between 1980 and 1997, the number of inmates in jails and prison tripled—increasing from .5 million to over 1.7 million [Gilliard & Beck 1998]. Women, most of whom are mothers of minor children, have particularly felt the effect of changing criminal justice policy [Bloom & Steinhart 1993]. One strategy of the war on drugs has been to use arrest and incarceration to reduce the demand for illegal drugs. At the same time that the number of women being arrested has increased, changes in sentencing laws have eliminated much of the discretion judges previously had to consider the need for mothers to care for young children when passing sentence [Raeder 1993; Bloom & Steinhart 1993]. Consequently, the number of women imprisoned for drug offenses increased more than fourfold (432%) between 1986 and 1991 alone [Snell 1994].

More than 75% of women in prison are mothers, each with an average of two children [Bloom & Steinhart 1993]. A smaller percentage of male prisoners—approximately 65%—are fathers [Snell 1994]. Children typically remain in their mothers' care before, during, and after the incarceration of a father. Johnston [1995] reports that approximately nine out of 10 children live with their mothers while their fathers are incarcerated. In comparison, a mother's incarceration is more disruptive to children, since mothers are frequently the primary caregivers for their children before being incarcerated [Bloom & Steinhart 1993]. Approximately 70% of children whose mothers are incarcerated live with grandparents and other relatives [Johnston 1995].

Relative Caregiver Characteristics

The National Council on Crime and Delinquency (NCCD) conducted a study of a small sample (N = 66) of caregivers of children whose mothers were incarcerated. The study found that most relative caregivers were maternal grandparents over age 50 with low-income levels [Bloom & Steinhart 1993]. These caregivers were caring for an average of 2.3 children who averaged 8.5 years of age. Forty-two percent of the children were African American, 25% were Latino, and 22% were Caucasian. Dressel and Barnhill [1990] estimate that caregivers not only care for their relatives' children, but many have "an uncounted number of older family members staying at the same residence."

Caregivers in the NCCD study identified problems encountered by the children in their care, including problems with learning/school (29%), behavior (27%), health/mental health (3.0%), substance abuse (3.0%), teen pregnancy (1.5%), and other areas (11%) [Bloom & Steinhart 1993]. Harm and Thompson [1995] found a higher incidence than did the NCCD study of reported school problems (38%, $N = 48$) and a similar incidence of reported behavior problems (24%).

A majority of caregivers report that their financial resources are inadequate to meet the necessary expenses of the children in their care [Bloom & Steinhart 1993; Harm & Thompson 1995; Phillips & Newell 1996]. Bloom & Steinhart [1993] found 44% of caregivers received AFDC, 43% supported children with their personal income, 11% received foster care payments, and 4.5% received child support. Harm and Thompson [1995] interviewed caregivers living primarily in rural communities. They found a similar incidence (44%) of caregivers receiving AFDC, a larger percentage of caregivers (20%) receiving child support, and a smaller percentage (16%) with income from employment. Social Security payments for the children were also a source of financial support for 11% of the caregivers studied by Harm and Thompson.

Caregivers commonly assume responsibility for children with an incarcerated parent through an informal arrangement between the parent and the caregiver. Only 13% of the caregivers interviewed by Harm and Thompson [1995] had been involved in court proceedings to obtain custody of the children. The majority of the caregivers (53%) were caring for the children before the children's mothers were incarcerated. Twenty-nine percent of the caregivers reported they took responsibility for the children at the time of the mother's arrest and a small number of relatives (4%) were caring for children who were born while their mother was incarcerated.

Support for Relative Caregivers

Unlike nonrelative foster parents who make the proactive choice to take responsibility for someone else's children, relative caregivers often enter into the caregiving role in the midst of a family crisis (e.g., an adult child abusing drugs, the arrest of an adult child, a grandchild being abused or neglected). And unlike nonrelative foster parents, relative caregivers find there is no systematic response to help them and the children in their care adjust to this major disruption in their lives.

Grandparents who become caregivers may blame themselves for their adult child's behavior. They may feel angry with their adult child for forcing them into the role of surrogate parents, grieve the loss of the "grandparenthood" they had anticipated, be anxious for the adult child's safety and well-being, and be ashamed of the fact that their adult child is incarcerated. Assuming responsibility for a relative's children can disrupt work, marriages, plans for retirement, and the lives of other children in the household.

While contending with their own emotions, caregivers must also help the children left in their care come to terms with their conflicting feelings about their parents. Children whose parents are incarcerated may feel abandoned and angry. They may think that they are somehow to blame for the parent's arrest. At the same time, they may be frightened for their parent and be anxious about their own future. As noted previously, children in the care of relatives may have academic, behavior, and emotional problems.

Caregivers need a broad array of supports.[1] They need information on how to manage problematic behaviors and access services for children that address such behaviors. They need information about what is happening with the children's parent: where the parent is, when she or he will be released, and when the child can visit. They need information about family law and child welfare policies to make informed decisions about their legal relationship to the children—decisions that may have potentially irreversible consequences. They may need housing as a result of their expanded household size or help negotiating with landlords to include the additional children in the terms of an existing lease. They may need transportation to gather all the documents needed to apply for social services or to take the children to visit their parents. Sometimes, caregivers just need a break.

Obstacles to Obtaining Support

Public assistance programs, including TANF, were not designed with relative caregivers in mind. Consequently, caregivers face many obstacles in accessing these programs [Mullens 1996]. When caregivers lack adequate financial means to meet the essential needs of children whose parents are incarcerated, siblings may be separated and disbursed among relatives. When the financial resources of those relatives are overtaxed, the children may be moved to the care of another relative. Harm and Thompson [1995] found that 29% of the children of imprisoned mothers they interviewed had been separated from their brothers and sisters.

Relatives caring for children whose parents are incarcerated often try to avoid involvement with the child welfare system for fear the children will be removed from their homes [Hungerford 1996; Phillips & Newell 1996]. Consequently, the primary source of assistance for many caregivers has been AFDC. Public policy changes, particularly the enactment of the Personal Responsibility and Work Opportunity Reconciliation Act of 1996 (P.L. 104-193), have dramatically increased the difficulties caregivers face. The act (1) ends AFDC and creates the Temporary Assistance to

Needy Families (TANF) program; (2) mandates that states give preference to placing children in out-of-home placements with relatives rather than strangers; (3) bans persons who have violated probation or parole from receiving TANF or food stamps; and (4) prevents persons convicted of certain drug felonies from receiving TANF or food stamps *for the rest of their lives.* These provisions may create obstacles to relatives caring for children while their mothers are incarcerated and make it more difficult for mothers to reunite with their children when they are released.[2]

Temporary Assistance to Needy Families (TANF)

Before the enactment of TANF, a significant percentage of relative caregivers relied on AFDC for support. The thrust of TANF, the successor of AFDC, is to move welfare recipients to work, yet employment may not be the compelling need of a relative caring for a child whose parent is incarcerated. The majority of caregivers (84%) interviewed by Harm and Thompson [1995] reported that assuming responsibility for children whose mothers were imprisoned caused major disruptions in their lives, one of which was having to quit their jobs. AFDC exempted persons from work requirements if they were too ill to work, over age 59, or needed in the home to care for an incapacitated household member. Under TANF, relatives who care for children while their parents are incarcerated face the same work requirements as would parents living with the children. TANF also limits the length of time a person may receive assistance, capping it at 60 cumulative months. If caregivers exhaust this lifetime limit while raising their own children or a relative's children, they are ineligible for assistance if they later assume responsibility for other related children. A review of 44 state welfare reform plans found that a number of states (Arkansas, Delaware, Florida, Georgia, Indiana, and New Mexico) set the maximum amount of time a person may receive assistance during their lifetime at less than the federal limit of 60 months [Children's Defense Fund 1997]. Other states (Arizona, California, Louisiana, Massachusetts, Montana, Ohio,

Oregon, South Carolina, Tennessee, Utah, and Virginia) have capped the number of consecutive months a person may receive assistance [Children's Defense Fund 1997].

Under AFDC, relatives could elect to be excluded from the assistance unit and apply for benefits for the children in their care as a separate assistance unit, relying only on the children's income to meet eligibility standards. Where caregivers can receive assistance for children as a "child only" case, the work requirements and lifetime limits would not apply to the caregiver. This would allow caregivers to receive TANF assistance for an extended period.

Receiving assistance through TANF is a bittersweet option for some relatives, who see the child welfare system providing greater support than they receive, both in terms of financial assistance and variety of services, to strangers to maintain children in out-of-home placements. They argue that if states are willing to pay strangers to care for children, they should be equally willing to provide comparable assistance to relatives with informal custody of children in the interest of preserving families [Phillips & Campbell 1997].

The Kinship Foster Care Preference

In addition to ending AFDC, the Personal Responsibility and Work Opportunity Reconciliation Act directs states to give preference to placing children with relatives rather than strangers when making out-of-home placements. On face value, formal kinship foster care appears to be an appealing avenue of support for children being cared for by relatives while parents are incarcerated. The average basic monthly foster care payment in nearly all states is greater than the average monthly AFDC child-only grant [Geen & Waters 1997]. In practice, however, formal foster care may inadvertently undermine families attempts to care for their relatives' children by unnecessarily expanding formal state control over a centuries-old tradition of informal care [Hornby et al. 1996; Testa 1996].

To receive foster care assistance, children must be in the custody of the state. This means that a grandparent or other relative—who may only need financial assistance and supportive services—may have to allege abuse or neglect against the parent. Ironically, even the fact that the parent left the children with the relative (a "nonlegally responsible adult") has been used to substantiate neglect.

Once children enter the formal foster care system, relatives have no certainty that their related children will be formally placed in their care. Even if the children are placed with the relative, the imperative of permanency may result in the termination of parental rights and the relative being asked to become an adoptive parent or face the possible removal of the children.

Caregivers' needs for support (e.g., financial assistance, transportation, housing, counseling, respite care, legal assistance, etc.) must be distinguished from the need of children for protective intervention [Hornby et al. 1996]. Resources must be made available to support caregivers in cases where there is no protective service interest in a child.

Recognizing the limitations of traditional foster care for children living with relatives, a number of states have created subsidized guardianship programs as an alternative permanency option for children in relative placements [Schwartz 1996].[3] Guardianship gives caregivers the legal authority to make important decisions about children. The subsidies provide needed financial support that can allow siblings to remain together in the same household and prevent the need for children to be moved from one relative's care to another's. Subsidized guardianship, however, comes into play only *after* children have been in foster care for varying lengths of time.

In Whose Best Interest?

The dramatic increase in the number of mothers being incarcerated in recent years has brought a growing recognition of the interplay between the criminal justice system, changing welfare legislation, and child welfare policy. While these areas of policy are often treated as if they were discrete and separate [Kordesh 1996], grandparents and other relatives caring for children whose parents are incarcerated know, perhaps better than anyone else, that the effects of these policies are interrelated. A grandmother participating in a support group describes her experience of this nexus of public policy as being "alone in a war."

Institutional and public policy reform will continue to be a challenge for those who are concerned about children whose parents are imprisoned and their caregivers. There is a growing recognition, however, that these children cannot be best served in isolation from their families and that helping to raise the visibility of these issues will perhaps prevent future generations from being swept into the criminal justice system.

Disruption of families due to parental incarceration is an increasingly prevalent problem. It often affects children in families with the fewest resources to cope with the stresses that come with the loss of a family member [Mustin 1994]. Throughout the United States, federal, state, and local governments are spending billions of dollars to build more prisons and jails. By getting tough on crime, the United States has also gotten tough on children. By getting tough on welfare recipients, policymakers may be placing children whose mothers are incarcerated at further disadvantage. The fundamental question for the child welfare community to raise about these changing policies is, Whose best interest do they serve? ◆

Notes

1. One way to help relative caregivers is to prepare mothers who are incarcerated to resume responsibility for their children when they are released. Policymakers have largely ignored the parenting role of women who are incarcerated. Mothers in jail and prison often lack access to resources such as parent education, drug treatment, psychological counseling, or employment training that could help them in fulfilling their roles as mothers [Johnston & Gabel 1995]. Without these resources, many mothers

will return to their children with the same problems they had before they were incarcerated.

2. A parent's criminal record creates obstacles to employment, public housing, and financial support. The Personal Responsibility and Work Opportunity Reconciliation Act adds to the difficulties mothers face in resuming responsibility for their children as it bans individuals who violate parole or probation orders from receiving assistance but makes no distinction between minor "technical violations" (e.g., missing an appointment), and more substantial violations (e.g., committing new crimes). Children will feel the repercussions of this provision that was intended to punish their mothers.

    Similarly, another punitive provision bans persons convicted of drug felonies from receiving TANF or food stamps for the rest of their lives. Given the increase in the number of mothers arrested for drug offenses, a significant number will be ineligible for assistance that could help them meet the economic needs of their children. This may pose an obstacle to mothers reuniting with their children and extend the length of time during which mothers are dependent on relatives to care for their children [Katz 1997].

3. Alaska, California, Colorado, Hawaii, Illinois, Massachusetts, Nebraska, New Mexico, South Dakota, and Washington.

References

Beatty, C., & Wilson, D. (1995, Summer). Legal guardianship: A stable, flexible option for real-world children and families. *Children's Voice, 4*(4), 8–10.

Bloom, B., & Steinhart, D. (1993). *Why punish the children: A reappraisal of the children of incarcerated mothers in America.* San Francisco: National Council on Crime and Delinquency.

Children's Defense Fund. (1997). *Selected features of welfare state plans.* Washington, DC: Author.

Dressel, P., & Barnhill, S. (1990). *Three generations at risk.* Atlanta, GA: Aid to Imprisoned Mothers.

Geen, R., & Waters, S. (1997). The impact of welfare reform on child welfare financing. In *New federalism—Issues and options for states (Series A. No. A–16).* Washington, DC: The Urban Institute.

Gilliard, D. K., & Beck, A. J. (1998). *Bureau of Justice Statistics bulletin: Prison and jail inmates at midyear 1997.* Washington, DC: U.S. Department of Justice, Bureau of Justice Statistics.

Harm, N., & Thompson, P. (1995). *Children of incarcerated mothers and their caregivers: A needs assessment*. Little Rock, AR: Centers for Youth and Families.

Hornby, H., Zeller, D., & Karraker, D. (1996). Kinship care in America: What outcomes should policy seek? *Child Welfare, 75*, 397–418.

Hungerford, G. (1996). Caregivers of children whose mothers are incarcerated: A study of the kinship placement system. *Children Today, 24*, 23–27.

Johnston, D. (1995). The care and placement of prisoners children. In K. Gabel & D. Johnston (Eds.), *Children of incarcerated parents* (pp. 103–123). New York: Lexington Books.

Johnston, D., & Gabel, K. (1995). Incarcerated parents. In K. Gabel & D. Johnston (Eds.), *Children of incarcerated parents* (pp. 3–20). New York: Lexington Books.

Katz, P. (1997). The effect of welfare reform on incarcerated mothers and their families, In *Family & Corrections Network Report*. Palmyra, VA: Family & Corrections Network.

Kordesh, R. (1996). Isolated decisions, severed families: Linking corrections and family policy in state government. In *Family & Corrections Network Report*. Palmyra, VA: Family and Corrections Network.

Mullens, F. (1996). *The effect of the Temporary Assistance for Needy Families Block Grant on grandparents raising grandchildren*. Washington, DC: AARP Public Policy Institute.

Mustin, J. (1994). Families of offenders: A key to crime prevention. In *Family & Corrections Network Report*. Palmyra, VA: Family and Corrections Network.

Phillips, S., & Campbell, R. (1997). *Rethinking child welfare assistance for children living with relatives other than their parents*. Little Rock, AR: Centers for Youth and Families.

Phillips, S., & Newell, D. (1996). *Report to the Little Rock Task Force on Youth*. Little Rock, AR: Centers for Youth and Families.

Raeder, M. (1993). "Gender neutral" sentencing wreaks havoc in the lives of women offenders and their children. *ABA Criminal Justice, 8*(20), 21–63.

Testa, M. (1996, September). *Home of Relative (HMR) reform in Illinois*. Kinship Care Forum conducted at the University of Illinois at Chicago, Jane Addams College of Social Work.

Snell, T. L. (1994). *Special report: Women in prison (NCJ–145321)*. Washington, DC: U.S. Department of Justice, Bureau of Justice Statistics.

Permanency Planning in the Context of Parental Incarceration: Legal Issues and Recommendations

4

Philip M. Genty

Parental incarceration is a growing problem that is not accommodated for in the traditional, time-driven model of permanency planning. The trend in both law and policy regarding children in out-of-home care is toward early termination of parental rights and placement for adoption. The federal Adoption and Safe Families Act of 1997 places additional pressure on state agencies to continue this trend. Child welfare agencies need to recognize the importance of maintaining parent-child relationships, even when a parent is incarcerated, and must develop creative approaches for dealing with the unique challenges presented by parental incarceration. The author, an advocate for incarcerated parents, offers recommendations for permanency planning in the context of parental incarceration.

Philip M. Genty, J.D., is Clinical Professor, School of Law, Columbia University, and Director, Prison and Families Clinic, New York, NY.

The increasing disruption of families through parental incarceration is challenging the child welfare community. No matter how deep the ties between parents and their children, the criminal justice system requires that family members be separated from each other for a considerable period of time. While achieving permanency for children in out-of-home care is an important goal, traditional time-driven notions of permanency planning may be inappropriate in cases involving parental incarceration. Strict, time-limited permanency planning policies fail to account for situations in which children and parents who have a strong attachment to each other are involuntarily separated for several years because of the parent's arrest and imprisonment.

For child welfare officials and case workers, and for parents, children, and caregivers, the increased incidence of parental incarceration calls for a reexamination of current policies and practices. Recently enacted federal legislation will have a profound impact on the way in which cases involving incarcerated parents are handled. This article describes some of these issues and suggest ways in which permanency planning might be approached in cases involving incarcerated parents.

Dimensions of the Problem

Over the past 15 years, the population of female prisoners has increased by almost 400%, while the male population has increased by more than 200% [U.S. Department of Justice 1995]. A large proportion of these prisoners are parents. In 1991, 67% of the state female prisoners in the United States had at least one child under the age of 18, and 63% of those women had more than one child. In 1991, 56% of male prisoners had children under the age of 18 [Snell 1994].

Imprisonment of a parent often disrupts intact families in which the parent and child know and are strongly attached to each other. In 1991, 72% of incarcerated mothers of minor children had lived with their children before entering prison. Among men, approximately one-half of the fathers of minor children reported that they had lived with their children prior to their imprisonment [Snell 1994].

The extent to which families with an incarcerated parent end up resorting to the child welfare system is difficult to measure. Surprisingly, neither child welfare agencies nor correctional officials compile this information on any systematic basis. A 1991 survey of state prisoners indicated that only 11% of the children of incarcerated women and 3% percent of the children of incarcerated men were in family foster homes or agency/institutional care [Snell 1994]. These data, however, likely understate the number of children in care because of the increased use of relatives as "kinship" foster parents. When responding to a survey that asks simply where their children are now living, many incarcerated parents whose children are in kinship foster care will, through embarrassment or incomplete knowledge, fail to disclose the foster care placement and report only that the children are with relatives. In the 1991 survey, 71% of the children of incarcerated mothers, and 13% of the children of incarcerated fathers, were with grandparents or other nonparent relatives; it is likely that a significant portion of these children were in kinship foster care placements [Snell 1994]. These data also show that incarcerated mothers must rely on nonparent caregivers for child care to a much greater extent than incarcerated fathers. Ninety percent of children of incarcerated fathers were being cared for by their mothers [Johnston 1995], but only 25% of children of incarcerated mothers were being cared for by their fathers [Snell 1994].

Legal Requirements

Reasonable Efforts

A parent's imprisonment does not change the basic legal requirements governing placement of children in out-of-home care. Agencies generally have a legal obligation to make "reasonable efforts" to preserve and strengthen the relationship between incarcerated parents and their children. The precise definition of "reasonable efforts" varies from state to state. For example, under California law, services to incarcerated parents and children may include paying the cost of collect phone calls between parent and child, and providing transportation, visiting, and other services to extended family members or foster parents providing care to the child. In addition, agencies must develop service plans in consultation with the parents and inform the parents of the rehabilitative services the parents are required to pursue. Rehabilitative services may include counseling, parenting classes, or vocational training programs, to the extent that such services are available in the prison [California Welfare & Institutions Code §361.5(e)].

Similarly, relevant New York law defines "diligent efforts" to incarcerated parents and their children as including:

> making suitable arrangements with a correctional facility and other appropriate persons for an incarcerated parent to visit the child within the correctional facility, if such visiting is in the best interests of the child...Such arrangements shall include, but shall not be limited to, the transportation of the child to the correctional facility, and providing or suggesting social or rehabilitative services to resolve or correct the problems, other than incarceration itself, which impair the incarcerated parent's ability to maintain contact with the child. [New York Social Services Law §384-b (7)(f)(5)]

Thus, parental incarceration does not, by itself, relieve an agency of the responsibility to provide services to parents and children. For the agencies, the most obvious challenges to facilitating a continued parent-child relationship relate to separation over time and distance. Increasing sentence lengths mean that parents and children are being kept apart for longer periods of time. In 1991, almost 60% of the women sentenced to state prison received maximum sentences of five years or more; more than

75% received sentences with a maximum of three years or more. For men, almost 75% received maximum sentences of five years or more [Snell 1994: 4].

A more accurate measure of the degree of family separation is the length of time actually served, because prisoners are typically paroled prior to the expiration of their maximum sentence. In 1992, women served an average of 15 months in state prisons (ranging from less than one year to seven years, depending on the offense and the race of the offender) [U.S. Department of Justice 1995: 573]. The overall mean was the same for African American and Caucasian women. Broken down by specific offenses, however, African American women served more time, sometimes by as much as 50%. In 1992, men served an average of 21 to 23 months in state prisons (ranging from less than one year to nine years, depending on the offense and the race of the offender). The overall mean and the means for most specific offenses were higher for African American men than for Caucasian men [U.S. Department of Justice 1995: 573]. These averages are likely to increase in the future as legislative efforts to eliminate or seriously limit parole result in more prisoners being required to serve most or all of their maximum sentences. At the same time, mandatory sentencing laws for certain crimes will lead to the imprisonment of even more parents.

The other important factor affecting the ability of agencies to provide services to incarcerated parents and their children is distance. As one commentator has noted:

This issue is particularly problematic for incarcerated mothers, because women's prisons are often located in rural areas that are inaccessible by public transportation. Also, there are fewer women's prisons across the country, so it is more likely that women will be placed farther from their homes. In one study, more than 60% of the children lived more than 100 miles away from their mothers. [Beatty 1997: 13, citing Bloom 1995]

Parental Fitness

Despite these formidable obstacles, the familial rights of parents and children are fundamental, and agencies must generally attempt to overcome them and to assist incarcerated parents and their children in maintaining a meaningful family relationship. Parental rights are not absolute, however, and not all cases involving incarcerated parents warrant the hard work and commitment of scarce resources required to nurture the parent-child relationship. In appropriate cases, the state may go to court to seek the permanent termination of parental rights. To do so, however, the state must prove that the parent is "unfit" [*Santosky v. Kramer* 1982; *Stanley v. Illinois* 1971].

A determination of "unfitness" is fact-specific and varies from case to case, but courts have consistently held that imprisonment, by itself, does not amount to parental unfitness [Genty 1991/92]. The parent's "fitness" must be measured by the parent's ability to "maintain a place of importance in the child's life" [*In re Adoption of Sabrina* 1984] .

The most obvious aspects of parental fitness are physical and financial, but family relationships and parental rights and responsibilities extend beyond these material considerations. For example, in the private sphere, it is recognized that children need to maintain contact with a noncustodial parent after parental divorce or separation [Garrison 1983]. This recognition is based on the understanding that a child's relationship with a parent has— in addition to the tangible qualities associated with physical care and presence—intangible qualities of love, affection, emotional support, and a sense of roots and identity. These intangible qualities are even more important when working with children in out-of-home care. Maintaining ties to parents may be crucial in such cases, because the children do not have the benefit of living with their other parent.

Two prisoners, longtime advocates for incarcerated mothers, described the importance to parents and children of maintaining family ties during incarceration:

We do not believe that incarcerated mothers and their children were sentenced to lose each other. Incarceration is an unfortunate setback for a mother and her child, and though children are not convicted of any crime, it is often they who suffer most. The fact that the mother has made a serious error does not negate motherhood, nor should it condemn children to lose their rights to the support and guidance of their mother. To profoundly disrupt family relations during the mother's imprisonment is to sentence the children to possible lifelong injury. [Bedell & Boudin 1993]

Recognizing the principle that parental incarceration does not automatically amount to unfitness, New Jersey's Supreme Court has articulated the factors that must be examined in determining whether an incarcerated parent's rights should be terminated:

evidence of the parent's performance as a parent before incarceration, including the extent to which the children were able to rely upon the parent; the parent's efforts to remain in contact with the children since incarceration; the parent's ability to communicate and visit with the children; the effect such communication and visitation will have on the children in terms of fulfilling the parental responsibility to provide nurture and emotional support, to offer guidance, advice and instruction, and to maintain an emotional relationship with the children; the risks posed to the children by the parent's criminal actions; the extent of the parent's rehabilitation during incarceration; the bearing of all of these factors on the parent-child relationship; the need of the children for permanency and stability and whether continuation of the parent-child relationship will undermine that need; and the effect that the continuation of the parent-child relationship will have on the psychological and emotional well-being of the children. [*Matter of Adoption of Children by L.A.S.* 1993]

Evaluating the fitness of an incarcerated parent in a termination of parental rights proceeding therefore requires that the court
conduct a full examination of the particular facts of the case. The
U.S. Supreme Court has held that this hearing must be held under a high evidentiary standard: parental unfitness must be
proven by "clear and convincing evidence," rather than the lower
standard of proof by a "preponderance of the evidence" [*Santosky
v. Kramer* 1982].

Thus, child welfare agencies must evaluate each case involving an incarcerated parent to determine whether a viable parent-
child relationship exists. For cases in which such a relationship is
absent, the issue of parental incarceration is largely irrelevant,
because preincarceration permanency planning was probably already geared toward termination of parental rights and adoption. Such cases might include those in which the parent was
chronically absent from the child's life due to incapacitation
through substance abuse. In those cases, the agency would simply proceed as if the parent had not been incarcerated.

For cases in which it is determined that a viable parent-child
relationship exists, however, the time of parental confinement
should be looked at as an interlude, during which the parental
ties can be nurtured and supported so that, to the greatest extent
possible, the parent-child relationship is as strong after the
parent's release as it was before [McGowan & Blumenthal 1978].
Other commentators have reached similar conclusions about the
importance to both the parent and the child of maintaining strong
family ties during the period of incarceration [Beckerman 1989;
Comment 1972; Driscoll 1985; Hale 1987; Kaslow 1987; Lowenstein
1986; Sack et al. 1976].

To do this, child welfare agencies must work within the context of the requirements being imposed upon the states by the
recently enacted Adoption and Safe Families Act of 1997 (P.L. 105-
89). In addition, child welfare agencies must develop specialized
approaches for meeting the challenges presented by parental incarceration.

The Adoption and Safe Families Act of 1997

The Adoption and Safe Families Act of 1997 (ASFA) amends the 1980 Adoption Assistance and Child Welfare Act (P.L. 96-272), the federal statute that provides for partial federal reimbursement to states for child welfare and out-of-home care expenses. To qualify for reimbursement, state child welfare and out-of-home care plans must comply with the requirements of the 1980 statute, as amended by ASFA. ASFA creates financial incentives to encourage adoptions [ASFA §201] and makes several other important changes.

Among the provisions of the 1980 act was the requirement that state child welfare agencies make reasonable efforts to preserve families by avoiding unnecessary out-of-home care placements and, where out-of-home care placement could not be avoided, by reunifying families as quickly as possible. ASFA modifies this "reasonable efforts" requirement in two respects. First, the statute establishes the "health and safety of the child" as the most important consideration in determining what family preservation and reunification efforts are required: "In determining reasonable efforts to be made with respect to a child...the child's health and safety shall be the paramount concern" [ASFA §101(a)(15)(A)]. ASFA also sets forth three exceptions to the reasonable efforts requirement:

(i) the parent has subjected the child to aggravated circumstances (as defined in State law, which definition may include but need not be limited to, abandonment, torture, chronic abuse, and sexual abuse; or
(ii) the parent has (committed or aided or abetted, attempted, conspired, or solicited the commission of) murder...or voluntary manslaughter...of another child of the parent...or felony assault that results in serious bodily injury to the child or another child of the parent; or
(iii) the parental rights of the parent to a sibling have been terminated involuntarily. [ASFA §101(a)(15)(D)]

ASFA does not preclude an agency from making reasonable efforts under these circumstances; it merely states that in such cases, such efforts "shall not be required to be made" [ASFA §101(a)(15)(D)]. Moreover, in other cases not encompassed within these exceptions, states continue to have a duty to provide preventive and reunification services to parents and children.

How much of an effect these changes to the reasonable efforts requirement will have in practice is unclear. Most state plans already allow agencies to dispense with reasonable efforts to preserve or reunify families in a given case when those efforts would be detrimental to the children's best interests. In addition, although the second exception applies directly to incarcerated parents who are imprisoned for crimes against children, agencies were almost certainly already forgoing reunification efforts in many, if not most, such cases.

In addition to modifying the reasonable efforts requirement, ASFA imposes new requirements about when termination of parental rights proceedings must be brought; it is these changes that are of greatest significance to incarcerated parents. The new law requires a state to file a petition to terminate the parent's rights, when a child "has been in foster care under the responsibility of the State for 15 of the most recent 22 months"; or a court has determined that the parent committed or aided or abetted, attempted, conspired, or solicited the commission of murder or voluntary manslaughter of another child of the parent or felony assault that results in serious bodily injury to the child or another child of the parent [ASFA §103(a)(3)]. The length of time a child is considered to have been in placement is calculated as follows: "A child shall be considered to have entered foster care on the earlier of (i) the date of the first judicial finding that the child has been subjected to child abuse or neglect; or (ii) the date that is 60 days after the date on which the child is removed from the home" [ASFA §103(b)(3)]. The statute also requires that a termination proceeding be brought when a court has found the child to be "an abandoned infant" [ASFA §103(a)(3)].

As with the reasonable efforts requirements, the requirement that a termination proceeding be initiated when a parent has been convicted of a violent crime against a child will probably not alter existing practice. A number of state statutes already provide for termination of parental rights of parents who have committed violent crimes against children [Genty 1991/92: 782–788].

The new provision mandating termination proceedings whenever a child has been in care for 15 of the past 22 months, however, is of potentially far-reaching consequences, particularly with respect to incarcerated parents. As noted above, in 1992, incarcerated women nationwide spent an average of 15 months in prison; for men, the average was almost two years [U.S. Department of Justice 1995]. The 1998 data for New York State are even more striking: 90% of the women in prison spend at least 18 months in prison, and 50% spend three or more years. For men the corresponding figures are 94% and 69% [New York State Department of Correctional Services 1998]. Thus, the new federal 15-month rule will mandate that termination proceedings be brought in the overwhelming majority of out-of-home care cases involving incarcerated parents.

Three exceptions set forth in the federal statute may somewhat lessen the effects of the statutory provisions. A termination of parental rights proceeding does not have to brought if:

(i) at the option of the State, the child is being cared for by a relative;
(ii) a State agency has documented in the case plan…a compelling reason for determining that filing such a petition would not be in the best interests of the child; or
(iii) the State has not provided to the family of the child, consistent with the time period in the State case plan, such services as the State deems necessary for the safe return of the child to the child's home, if reasonable efforts…are required to be made with respect to the child. [ASFA §103(a)(3)]

The last of these exceptions requires a state agency to admit that it has not done its job properly; it therefore seems unlikely that it will be widely used. The first two exceptions, however, provide agencies with a necessary degree of flexibility. For a case in which the parent is serving a lengthy prison sentence but has relatives available to care for the child, a state may use placement with the relative to avoid the strict, adoption-oriented requirements of the federal statute. Even in a case where no relative is available, a state agency may avoid the time-limited permanency planning requirements by carefully documenting in the case plan that severance of the parent-child relationship would be contrary to the child's best interests. These two important exceptions make it possible for state agencies to continue to work with incarcerated parents, their children, and the caregivers to preserve and strengthen family relationships.

While the effects of ASFA upon child welfare practices and procedures are likely to be significant, ASFA will operate within the framework of case law defining the rights of parents. ASFA compels a state agency to bring a termination of parental rights proceeding under a number of circumstances, but the mere requirement that such a proceeding be brought does not mean that the proceeding will necessarily result in the termination of the parent's rights. Termination proceedings will still be subject to the constitutional requirement that the parent be proven "unfit" by clear and convincing evidence [*Santosky v. Kramer* 1982]. ASFA will undoubtedly result in greater numbers of termination proceedings being brought, but many of these will ultimately be dismissed for lack of proof of parental unfitness.

Meeting the Challenge of Permanency Planning in Cases Involving Parental Incarceration

Child welfare officials can prepare to work within the requirements imposed by ASFA by developing specialized strategies for dealing with cases of parental incarceration. Some preliminary suggestions for approaches to permanency planning in the context of parental incarceration follow.

Identify the Caseload of Children

Identifying the caseload of children of incarcerated parents seems like an obvious suggestion, but a significant difficulty in developing legal and policy approaches for handling these cases is the lack of reliable data. Child welfare agencies do not routinely compile this information, so it is impossible to say with certainty how many cases in a given county involve children of incarcerated parents. Specialized approaches cannot be developed without this information.

Determine the Viability of the Parent-Child Relationship

Because the resources needed to work effectively with incarcerated parents and their children are scarce, agencies must first determine which cases warrant such efforts and document their reasoning in the case records.

This "triaging" has taken on additional importance because of the timelines established by ASFA. As noted earlier, the federal statute requires that termination of parental rights proceedings be brought for any child who has been in care for 15 of the past 22 months. This requirement can be avoided, however, if "a State agency has documented in the case plan ... a compelling reason for determining that filing such a petition would not be in the best interests of the child" [ASFA §103(a)(3)]. Thus, where an agency has determined that a viable parent-child relationship exists, the agency must carefully document its findings in the case record so that it may continue to work with the incarcerated parent and the child without violating the federal requirements. In addition, because these are the considerations that a court would make in determining whether parental "unfitness" has been proven by clear and convincing evidence, a state agency may, by documenting these factors in the case record, avoid being required by ASFA to initiate time-consuming termination proceedings that will ultimately be dismissed.

Recruit Relatives Caregivers and Provide Necessary Resources and Services

Another exception to ASFA's strict time limits is that termination of parental rights proceedings need not be instituted for children who are being cared for by relatives [ASFA §103(a)(3)]. Thus, efforts to recruit relatives as caregivers have taken on greater importance in cases involving incarcerated parents. Once relatives are found, they must be provided with the financial resources they need to enable the children to maintain contact with their parents (e.g., money to make regular phone calls), and the therapeutic services necessary to help the children deal with their parents' incarceration.

Develop Specialized Units of Case Workers

One of the most serious obstacles to the continuation of a family relationship during parental incarceration is the geographical distance that separates parents and children, due to the placement of correctional facilities in remote rural locations [Bloom 1995; Human Rights Watch 1996]. The geographical distance means that parents and children have little or no physical contact with each other. A 1991 survey revealed that fewer than 20% of incarcerated parents saw their children as often as once a month, and 50% never saw their children [Snell 1994].

For child welfare agencies, the obstacles to providing regular visiting with incarcerated parents are considerable. The typical agency case worker may have one case involving an incarcerated parent out of a much larger caseload. For a single visit to prison, however, the case worker will likely have to devote an entire day. In addition, for the children involved, the visit will involve a long and tedious car ride.

One potential solution is to develop specialized units of case workers to work exclusively with children whose parents are incarcerated. In that way, several visits could be scheduled on the same day, and a group of children could be transported by bus to the prison. Other solutions will need to be devised for parents who are in prisons located at a distance that makes a day trip impossible. Case workers working in these specialized units may be able to recruit families in the communities surrounding the prisons to provide overnight lodging for the children.

Similarly, children of incarcerated parents require specialized services to help them deal with their parents' imprisonment [Johnston 1995; Kampfner 1995]. These service needs may be unique to children of incarcerated parents, and the typical case worker will not have the knowledge and experience necessary to provide or locate these services. Here also, specialized units devoted to children of incarcerated parents might provide some answers. Such units could bring children of incarcerated parents together for group sessions. The children might also be taken to the prison for family therapy with their parents.

In some localities, the small size of the caseload makes the creation of specialized units impractical. Designated case workers, however, can receive specialized training to enable them to deal with cases involving parental incarceration.

Conclusion

The trend toward incarceration of greater numbers of people for longer periods of time shows no signs of abating. As a result, an increasing portion of agencies' out-of-home care caseloads will likely involve children of incarcerated parents. Traditional notions of permanency planning, however, do not fit cases of parental incarceration, as they fail to take account of the strong ties that may exist between parents and children who are involuntarily separated for lengthy periods of time because of the parents' imprisonment. Effective family work in cases involving parental incarceration requires a significant expenditure of time and energy, and child welfare agencies should identify the cases where such efforts would be successful in maintaining and strengthening viable parent-child relationships. In such cases, agencies must develop new permanency planning approaches, consistent with the requirements of ASFA, for families in which a parent is incarcerated. For many children of incarcerated parents, the best permanency plan is one in which the parent continues to play a significant role in the child's life. ◆

References

Adoption of Children by L.A.S., Matter of, 134 N.J. 127, 143–144 (1993).

Adoption of Sabrina, In re, 325 Pa. Super. 17, 472 A.2d 624, 627 (Super. Ct. 1984).

Bloom, B. (1995). Incarcerated mothers. In K. Gabel & D. Johnston (Eds.), *Children of incarcerated parents* (pp. 21–30). New York: Lexington Books. *Cited in* Beatty, C. (1997). *Parents in prison: Children in crisis* (p. 13). Washington, DC: CWLA Press.

Beckerman, A. (1989). Incarcerated mothers and their children in foster care: The dilemma of visitation. *Children and Youth Services Review, 11,* 175–183.

Bedell, P., & Boudin, K. (1993). *The foster care handbook for incarcerated parents: A manual of your legal rights and responsibilities.* New York: Bedford Hills Correctional Facility.

California Welfare & Institutions Code §361.5(e).

Comment. (1972). The prisoner-mother and her child. *Capital University Law Review, 1,* 127–144.

Driscoll, D. (1985, August). Mother's Day once a month. *Corrections Today, 47,* 18–24.

Garrison, M. (1983). Why terminate parental rights? *Stanford Law Review, 35,* 423, 455–472.

Genty, P. (1991/92). Procedural due process rights of incarcerated parents in termination of parental rights proceedings: A fifty state analysis. *Journal of Family Law, 34,* 757–846.

Hale, D. (1987). The impact of mothers' incarceration on the family system: Research and recommendations. *Marriage and Family Review, 12,* 143–154.

Human Rights Watch, Women's Rights Project. (1996). *All too familiar: Sexual abuse of women in U.S. prisons.* New York: Author.

Hairston, C. F., & Hess, P. M. (1989, April). Family ties: Maintaining child-parent bonds is important. *Corrections Today, 51,* 102–106.

Johnston, D. (1995). Effects of parental incarceration. In K. Gabel & D. Johnston (Eds.), *Children of incarcerated parents* (pp. 59–88). New York: Lexington Books.

Kampfner, C. (1995). Post-traumatic stress reactions in children of incarcerated mothers. In K. Gabel & D. Johnston (Eds.), *Children of incarcerated parents* (pp. 89–100). New York: Lexington Books.

Kaslow, F. (1987). Couples or family therapy for prisoners and their significant others. *The American Journal of Family Therapy, 15,* 352–360.

Lowenstein, A. (1986, January). Temporary single parenthood—The case of prisoners' families. *Family Relations, 35,* 79, 84.

McGowan, B. G., & Blumenthal, K. L. (1978). *Why punish the children? A study of children of women prisoners.* Hackensack, NJ: National Council on Crime and Delinquency.

New York Social Services Law §384-b(7)(f)(5).

New York State Department of Correctional Services. (1998, June). Statistics from Division of Support Operations, Albany, NY (unpublished).

Sack, W. H., Seidler, J., & Thomas, S. (1976). Children of imprisoned parents: A psychosocial exploration. *American Journal of Orthopsychiatry, 46,* 618–628.

Santosky v. Kramer, 455 U.S. 745 (1982).

Stanley v. Illinois, 405 U.S. 645 (1971).

Snell, T. L. (1994). *Special Report: Women in prison.* Washington, DC: U.S. Department of Justice, Bureau of Justice Statistics.

U.S. Department of Justice. (1995). *Sourcebook of criminal justice statistics 1995.* Washington, DC: U.S. Department of Justice, Bureau of Justice Statistics.

Girl Scouts Beyond Bars: Facilitating Parent-Child Contact in Correctional Settings

5

Kathleen J. Block and Margaret J. Potthast

Distant prison locations, inconvenient visiting schedules, and the negative effects of a mother's imprisonment on her children often complicate the child welfare professional's work with the children of incarcerated mothers. Enhanced prison visiting programs offer a mechanism to support the mother-child relationship, facilitate reunification efforts, and assist with permanency planning. This article discusses one such program, *Girl Scouts Beyond Bars*, in relation to the problem of mother-child separation via imprisonment; traditional visiting practices; and the issues confronting child welfare professionals serving the children of imprisoned mothers.

Kathleen J. Block, Ph.D., is Associate Professor, Division of Criminology, Criminal Justice, and Social Policy; and Margaret J. Potthast, Ph.D., is Assistant Professor, Division of Applied Psychology and Quantitative Methods, University of Baltimore, Baltimore, MD.

L ess than three decades ago, the number of women in state and federal prisons serving sentences of one year or more was estimated at about 6,000; by 1997, the number had grown to more than 70,000 [Gilliard & Beck 1998; Mumola & Beck 1997]. As has long been the case, the majority of incarcerated women are young, single, economically disadvantaged women of color with children [McGowan & Blumenthal 1978; Grossman 1984; Feinman 1986; Chesney-Lind 1992; Hungerford 1993]. Prior to their incarceration, most were the primary caregivers for their children [Grossman 1984; Feinman 1986; Hungerford 1993] and hoped to reunite with them upon their release [McGowan & Blumenthal 1978; Datesman & Cales 1983; Grossman 1984; Baunach 1985; Bloom & Steinhart 1993]. Most children of incarcerated women live with relatives during the prison period; however, some are placed in out-of-home care [Grossman 1984; McGowan & Blumenthal 1978; Hungerford 1993; Baunach 1985; Bloom & Steinhart 1993].

Whether locating services for the families of incarcerated persons, helping to maintain contact between parents and children, developing permanency plans, or facilitating family reunification, child welfare professionals who work with children with incarcerated parents find their responsibilities complicated by the mothers' incarceration [Beatty 1997]. Prison regulations regarding communication and visiting, and the often distant location of correctional facilities, impede routine communication and interaction. Lengthy prison terms and the emotional effects of imprisonment on mothers and their children threaten their relationships and affect permanency plans and reunification possibilities. Yet within this context, child welfare professionals confront decisions regarding the children's short-term and long-term placements.

Several states have developed enhanced prison visiting programs for inmate mothers and their children. These programs may offer child welfare professionals a mechanism with which they can support the mother-child relationship, facilitate reunification where that is an option, and assist with permanency planning. One such program is *Girl Scouts Beyond Bars* (GSBB), begun in Maryland in 1992 and in operation today in at least 12 states [Moses 1995].[1] This article describes the *Girl Scouts Beyond Bars* program in relation to the children of incarcerated parents, the effects of incarceration on the mother-child relationship, traditional prison visiting practices, and the issues confronting child welfare professionals working with this population.

Mothers in Prison

Imprisonment impacts mothers, their children and their relationships in a variety of ways. Some mothers grieve the "loss" of their child [Hairston & Lockett 1985] and experience guilt and lowered self-esteem as a parent [Radish 1994; Baunach 1982, 1985; McGowan & Blumenthal 1978; Hairston & Lockett 1985]. Most inmate mothers attempt to remain close to their children through letters and phone calls [Datesman & Cales 1983; Bloom & Steinhart 1993]. Many report difficulties in maintaining their relationships with their children, however, because of infrequent communication and limited or no prison visits. The women feel helpless to control their children's welfare [Hairston & Lockett 1985; Baunach 1982, 1985; McGowan & Blumenthal 1978; Bloom & Steinhart 1993]. Anxious about postprison reunification [Datesman & Cales 1983; Stanton 1980], many fear that their children may resent them, or that their children may bond too well with their caregivers [Baunach 1985]. Ultimately, they worry that their relationship with their children will have disintegrated by the end of the incarceration period [Rocheleau 1987; Bloom & Steinhart 1993].

Despite many shared experiences while imprisoned, inmate mothers are not a homogeneous group with respect to their prior living situations with their children [Bloom & Steinhart 1993]. Baunach [1985] describes preprison mother-child relationships as ranging from neglectful or absent to warm and nurturing. LeFlore and Holston [1989] found inmate mothers to possess positive parenting attitudes (love, caring, guidance) equivalent to those of mothers who are not incarcerated. Indeed, the vast majority of mothers in that study felt that they were successful parents. In some cases in which prior attachment is missing, imprisonment provides an opportunity for mothers to establish a relationship with their children. After studying mothers in Bedford Hills Correctional Institution, Clark [1995: 309] observed:

> Throughout my research, I was struck by the contradictory ways in which women talk about the role that prison plays in their lives and relationships with their children. On the one hand, they describe prison as oppressive, belittling, deprivational, and destructive of mother-child bonds. On the other hand, many women say that prison saved them, that their relationships with their children were jeopardized long before they came to prison, and that they have been able to understand themselves and improve their relationships with their children while in prison. It seems that both are true.

When asked what would help them become better mothers upon release, inmate mothers in Ohio outlined a child visiting program with prolonged visits and close interaction with their children that would allow the mothers to take responsibility for their activities [Hungerford 1993]. "Taking responsibility" for activities is not a typical inmate role; however, it is stressed as an important role for inmate mothers to be able to play with their children to strengthen their relationships [Clark 1995; Bloom & Steinhart 1993].

Children of Incarcerated Mothers

While the exact number of children of incarcerated mothers is unknown, estimates placed it at 1.5 million children in 1994 [Johnston 1994]. When mothers before their incarceration play a minimal role in their children's lives, or are completely absent, their imprisonment may have little or no effect on their children [Gabel 1992]. When separation by prison is the first break in a strong and nurturing relationship, however, or another disruption in a long series of traumas, the consequences can be devastating [Bloom & Steinhart 1993; Adalist-Estrin 1994; Johnston 1994]. Many children experience feelings of abandonment, loneliness, sadness, anger, and resentment at their parent's incarceration [McGowan & Blumenthal 1978; Henriques 1982; Hungerford 1993]. Eating and sleeping disorders may arise [Rocheleau 1987], as well as diminished academic performance, disruptive behavior at home or school, and feelings of being stigmatized [Stanton 1980; Zalba 1964; Henriques 1982; Hungerford 1993]. Many children express anxiety about prison visits and worry about their parent's return after prison [Stanton 1980; Hungerford 1993]. The children's home lives are considerably disrupted by imprisonment, through placement with new caregivers, separation from siblings, or relocation [Stanton 1980; Fritsch & Burkhead 1982; Zalba 1964; McGowan & Blumenthal 1978; Henriques 1982; Hungerford 1993].

Visiting Mothers in Prison

Clark [1995] describes many children as going to great lengths to see their mothers in prison. Since most children cannot transport themselves to visit their mothers, however, they must rely on their caregivers or another person for transportation. Visits are often infrequent because prisons may be located far from home, and caregivers may be unable or unwilling to transport children to the prison for a visit [Kiser 1991; Hadley 1981; Henriques 1982; Feinman 1986; Hungerford 1993]. Bloom and Steinhart [1993] found that 54% of the mothers in the nine prisons they studied had received no visits from their children. They also found that the mothers' living situations before their incarceration made a difference. Whereas 54% of the mothers who lived with their children before prison received at least one visit from them, only 28% of those who did not live with their children before prison received a visit. Some caregivers refuse to help children visit, perceiving the institutional setting as too severe and frightening or, in some cases, as too much like a "country club" and not frightening enough [Datesman & Cales 1983]. Others believe that the mother is an unhealthy influence on the child and deny visits to discourage their relationship [Bloom & Steinhart 1993]. In contrast, some caregivers will extend themselves considerably to ensure that children can visit their mothers [Fuller 1993].

When regular prison visits do occur, standard visiting practices in most prisons exacerbate the anxieties experienced by incarcerated parents and their young children [Bloom & Steinhart 1993; Johnston 1994]. Typical visiting rooms are uncomfortable and inappropriate for children. They are settings for adult conversation, providing little opportunity for meaningful communication between children and their mothers [Simon & Landis 1991; Baunach 1982; Logan 1992; Bloom & Steinhart 1993]. Nevertheless, many mothers feel that the benefits of visits outweigh their negative aspects. As one mother stated:

> The main advantages of the visits are tightening up the relationship, watching your children grow, your children watching you grow, how you've changed, being able to love one another. [Datesman & Cales 1983: 147]

Recognizing these problems, several women's prisons have developed specialized visiting programs to normalize the interaction of mothers and children by providing play areas, making available children's toys and activities, and permitting extended contact visits with flexible scheduling. Some facilities arrange for busing the children to the prisons [Clement 1993]. Neto and Bainer [1983] observe that it is not uncommon for a prison with extended visiting for children to structure the extended visits as a program.

The Girl Scouts Beyond Bars Program

In 1992, Maryland's Correctional Institution for Women (MCIW) partnered with the Girl Scouts of Central Maryland (GSCM) to establish a unique enhanced visiting program for inmate mothers and their daughters,[2] a program that has since served as a model for the GSBB programs in other states. While each *Girl Scouts Beyond Bars* program comprises unique features, partnerships, program services, funding sources, and challenges, the programs share common objectives and practices. GSBB's objectives are to provide enhanced visiting between mothers and daughters so as to preserve or enhance the mother-daughter relationship, to reduce the stress of separation, to enhance the daughter's sense of self, to reduce reunification problems, and, ultimately, to help decrease the likelihood of the mother's failure in the community. To achieve these objectives, the programs provide door-to-door transportation of the daughters to the mother's facility for regularly scheduled troop meetings, and involve both mothers and daughters in traditional Girl Scout activities. In most programs, the girls participate in other Girl Scout activities as well, such as community troop meetings and field trips. Many programs hold or require parenting programs for the mothers, and offer counseling and other services for the daughters.

Maryland's GSBB program was designed to accommodate a maximum of 30 mothers and 40 daughters. To qualify as troop members, inmates had to have a daughter between the ages of 7 and 17 living in Baltimore City, have 12 months remaining on their sentences, be infraction free for 30 days, remain infraction free, and not have a conviction for an offense against children. Mothers' memberships end upon their release from MCIW; their daughters, however, may remain in the community troop.

GSBB holds three types of meetings for participants: a two-hour troop meeting in MCIW with mothers and daughters, a mothers' meeting, and a community troop meeting for daughters. Twice a month, on alternate Saturday mornings, the inmate mothers meet to discuss parenting concerns and plan troop activities. Shortly after, the troop meets in the prison gymnasium. In addition, twice per month on alternate Saturdays, community meetings are held for the daughters.

Troop meetings begin with 15 minutes of private conversation between the mothers and their daughters, followed by the Girl Scout pledge and various structured troop activities. Mothers and daughters work on badges, develop special projects, and discuss issues confronting girls today, such as teen pregnancy and drug use. Led by a licensed social worker, a GSBB staff member, or a volunteer, the mothers' meetings focus on child-rearing issues and GSBB program plans. During the girls' community meetings, the Scouts work on projects begun in MCIW or initiate projects to take into MCIW. Supplementing the meetings, the staff and volunteers provide the girls with activities enjoyed by other Girl Scout troops, such as sleepovers, field trips, and multitroop gatherings.

Transporting the girls to and from the various meetings is a central component of GSBB. Each Saturday on which there is a meeting, two buses provide door-to-door service for the daughters, who are contacted during the week by GSBB staff. The caregivers' task is to have the girls ready and waiting. For GSCM, the logistics and the costs of transportation are a substantial portion of the GSBB effort. The program budget is approximately $30,000 per year.

In 1996, the authors concluded a two-year study of Maryland's GSBB program, examining program operations, objectives, and outcomes with respect to enhanced visiting, and the benefits for the mothers and daughters.[3] In brief, the study found that GSBB increases and improves the quality of mother-daughter visits, and helps to preserve or enhance the mother-daughter bond. In addition, there is evidence that GSBB may enhance the daughters' sense of self and reduce some of their separation problems.

GSBB Mothers and Daughters

Surveys of the MCIW resident population conducted in 1991 and 1992 by the Maryland Governor's Office for Children, Youth and Families suggest that MCIW was an appropriate setting for this program. More than 80% of the MCIW inmates were the mothers of at least one child. A third of their children were less than 6 years old, and 55% were 6 to 18 years old. Three-fourths of the mothers lived with their children prior to entering prison, and 69% of the mothers had primary caregiver responsibility. Almost all planned to reunite with their children upon their release. Twenty percent of the children lived with their fathers and another 60% lived with their grandparents or other relatives. The rest were cared for by nonrelatives, or were in family foster care. The majority of mothers reported that their children reacted negatively to their mothers' incarceration, experiencing emotional, behavioral, or school problems. Thirty percent reported that they had no personal contact with their children while incarcerated. Forty percent communicated with their children through telephone calls and letters. Slightly more than a third received fewer than one visit per month from them.

The GSBB mothers were very similar to the MCIW mothers surveyed. Because of the program's focus on mothers of minor children from Baltimore City, the GSBB mothers were slightly younger (average age of 29) and more were African American (90% versus 45%) than in the MCIW population as a whole. Additionally, more GSBB mothers were or had been married (59% versus 38%), lived with their children immediately prior to their imprisonment (86% versus 74%), and claimed primary child care responsibilities for their children (73% versus 69%). Finally, whereas 94% of the MCIW mothers stated that they planned to reunite with their children after their incarceration ended, 100% of the GSBB mothers anticipated such a reunion.

The daughters in the program were 1 to 16 years old when their mothers entered prison. For 70% of the girls interviewed, their current separation was the first caused by their mother's incarceration. Slightly more than 80% said that their mother was their primary caregiver prior to her incarceration; another 7% named their mother and father. All said that they expected to be reunited with their mothers after prison. During their mothers' incarceration, all of the girls interviewed lived with relatives, and most (79%) lived with at least some of their siblings. Two-thirds lived with the same caregiver throughout the incarceration period. A few daughters not interviewed were in family foster care at some point during their program involvement.

Most of the interviewed caregivers had been an integral part of the mothers' and daughters' lives prior to the mother's incarceration, the majority living with them. The others assumed the daughter's care when the mother entered MCIW, intervening at the mother's request or to keep the girl out of the out-of-home care system. More than 85% of the mothers, daughters, and caregivers reported that the mothers and daughters communicated with one another prior to their involvement in GSBB, most commonly through phone calls and letters. The majority of daughters visited their mothers before joining GSBB; in most cases, they were taken to prison by a caregiver or close relative. In prison, the daughters visited their mothers accompanied by the person who provided the transportation.

Seventy percent of the mothers and 52% of the caregivers reported that the daughters suffered emotional problems (depression, sadness, anger); behavioral problems (withdrawal, crying, bed-wetting, rudeness, fighting, disobedience); and school problems (lowered grades, disobedience, suspension) in response to their mothers' incarceration. A few received professional counseling for their problems. The daughters who did not experience difficulties were said to be too young at the time, simply "well-adjusted," or "used to it" because the mother had been in MCIW previously. One caregiver said that the daughter was a bit sad, but that her living situation was better during her mother's incarceration than it was before.

The interviews with current and former GSBB members included standardized measures and questions to assess the mother-daughter relationship, the daughter's self-concept, the daughter's behavioral problems, and the mother's separation anxiety.[4] The Hudson Parent-Child Contentment Scale [Hudson 1982] scores reveal positive feelings between the mothers and daughters, suggesting the presence of a strong mother-daughter bond. The scores are highest on the items referencing liking one another, enjoying each other's company, and trusting one another. On the downside, some daughters expressed occasional embarrassment regarding their mothers, and some mothers felt that they needed more patience and understanding with their daughters.

As measured by the Piers-Harris Children's Self-Concept Scale [Piers 1984], most of the girls' overall self-concepts fell within a normal range. A few girls' scores were very low, however, suggesting the presence of clinically low self-esteem. The mothers' and caregivers' assessments of the girls' behavior patterns via the Conner's Parent Rating Scale [Conners 1990] complement the Piers-Harris data in profiling the group as "average" overall. The girls were profiled as being slightly more impulsive than average, however, and slightly more likely to exhibit conduct problem behaviors than other girls their age. A small number of girls was seen as having a variety of behavioral problems.

Using Fessler's Worry Scale [Fessler 1991], the study found that the imprisoned mothers' main worries concerned their daughters' feelings (anger, missing mother); certain aspects of their daughters' living situations (schooling, friends); and their ability to support their daughters after prison. Fewer mothers expressed substantial concerns about their daughters' home situations, the daughters' affection for their mothers, and desire to communicate with their mothers in prison. These scores suggest that the mothers are confident in their relationship with their daughters, yet they worry about the emotional harm that they may have caused their daughters and the mother-daughter relationship.

Overall, the girls and mothers in GSBB are fairly representative of children of incarcerated mothers and inmate mothers studied previously. Although they experience separation problems,
the lives of the majority of girls are normalized by remaining
within their families; they enjoy stable routines, positive self-
concepts and strong mother-daughter bonds. Given that the study
was undertaken after the mothers and daughters joined the program, it is unclear whether the program prompted the positive
relationships or supported those already in place.

Program Outcomes

Analysis of visiting data and interview data revealed that GSBB
enhanced regular prison visits. Comparing the visiting records
of GSBB mothers with those of a matched group who met the
criteria for membership but did not participate, it was found that
a higher percentage of GSBB mothers (64%) received visits from
their daughters than did the matched group (49%) and averaged
more visits per year (mean = 11.6 versus 6.1, median = 6.9 versus
3). On average, the GSBB mothers received visits from their
daughters during almost half of the months available, while the
matched group received visits in slightly more than 30% of them.

As to whether GSBB replaced or supplemented regular visits, an examination of the regular visiting patterns of GSBB members before, during, and after GSBB program participation indi-
cates that for most mothers receiving visits from their daughters,
GSBB visits are supplemental. Significant correlations between
the number of visits per month before joining GSBB and the number of visits during the program and after the program reflect a
consistency in the visiting patterns that is relatively untouched
by GSBB participation. Consistent with this finding, the majority
of interviewed mothers (53%) stated that participation in GSBB
had no effect on their daughters' regular visiting patterns. The
rest stated that the program either brought their daughters closer
emotionally and increased their regular visits (27%) or substituted

for regular visits, which declined once GSBB participation began (21%). For the 36% of mothers who received no regular visits from their daughters, GSBB participation provided their only visits.

Sixteen mothers and 13 daughters completed the Hudson Parent-Child Contentment Scale twice, and six mothers and four daughters completed it three times, at roughly six-month intervals. The mean scores remained consistently high across the three waves of interviews and did not change significantly, suggesting the presence of a strong and stable mother-daughter bond. According to the caregivers interviewed, however, GSBB significantly improved the daughter's relationship with her mother: either they bonded for the first time, or they retained or strengthened the bond interrupted by incarceration. Caregivers described improved communication and understanding between the daughters and their mothers, and a greater desire to be together. Daughters who were disinterested in visits prior to GSBB became excited about them after joining. Two caregivers said, essentially, that "the visits are enjoyable now."

Virtually all caregivers described some decrease in the daughters' problems that had been caused by their mothers' incarceration. Caregivers described the daughters as less sad, angry, or worried about their mothers, and less afraid that their mothers would be lost to them. According to the caregivers, the daughters fought less and "sassed" teachers less. Eight caregivers mentioned that the girls' school grades improved, though a ninth mentioned that the grades fell after joining GSBB.

As viewed by the caregivers, additional positive effects on the daughters stemmed more from the activities of GSBB itself than from spending time with their mothers. A few caregivers described the daughters as becoming less shy and as building self-esteem through their interactions with other girls. Almost all girls (92%) reported that they made new friends in the Girl Scouts, and half said that they contacted them outside the meetings.

Applications for Child Welfare Professionals

The findings from the Maryland study suggest that the *Girl Scouts Beyond Bars* program is beneficial for inmate mothers and their daughters in that it enhances visiting, supports mother-daughter relationships, and may help to ease some of the problems caused by incarceration. In fulfilling these objectives, the *Girl Scouts Beyond Bars* program and other similar enhanced visiting programs may facilitate the child welfare professional's work with incarcerated mothers and their children. The situations in which these programs may be useful are numerous and varied.

In one scenario, the mother, daughter, and caregiver may have strong bonds but lack the means to maintain the direct, personal contact required for reunification. In another scenario, the mother's incarceration may extend beyond the child's status as a minor, so the child welfare professional confronts issues of long-term guardianship or adoption and the mother's role in the child's life. In a third scenario, the mother-child relationship may be troubled, but the relatively short prison term foretells the likelihood of reunification. In these, and in other scenarios, the child welfare professional's responsibilities include helping to maintain contact between the parent and child, providing services to the family, developing permanency plans, and/or facilitating reunification. Communicating with mothers, and supporting regular visits by children, promote these objectives and may be necessary. Encouraging qualifying children and mothers to participate in available programs of this type benefits those involved.

At the organizational level, child welfare agencies that have not already done so might consider establishing linkages with enhanced visiting programs serving their communities. The *Girl Scouts Beyond Bars* programs, for example, involve a variety of organizational partnerships, some offering a range of community-based services along with their prison programs. These programs generally welcome the support and involvement of others working with children. For the child welfare agency, such involvement can broaden the network of programs and agencies available to serve incarcerated children, thus optimizing their use of resources and maximizing the ability of child welfare professionals to reach their goals successfully. ◆

Notes

1. GSBB programs are in Arizona, California, Delaware, Florida, Kentucky, Massachusetts, Missouri, New Jersey, North Carolina, Ohio, Pennsylvania, and Texas. GSBB programs are under consideration or are in the planning stages in several other jurisdictions.

2. The Girl Scouts' investment in this program is consistent with its expanding mission. Begun in 1912, the Girl Scouts defined its mission as helping girls to develop to their full potential, and to mature into competent and resourceful women. In the last decade, it directed some of its attention to young people living in high-risk areas. Through its National Center for Innovation, for example, it experimented with facility-based programs in public housing community centers [Task Force on Youth Development and Community Programs 1992]. GSBB is another, but perhaps even more unique, facility-based Girl Scout program for high-risk youths.

3. Research on the GSBB Program in Maryland was supported under award #94-IJ-CX-K013 from the National Institute of Justice, Office of Justice Programs, U.S. Department of Justice. Points of view in this document are those of the authors and do not necessarily represent the official position of the U.S. Department of Justice. In the study, researchers collected data from GSCM and MCIW records, and from interviews of GSBB participants (mothers, daughters, and caregivers), and GSBB providers (leaders, staff, and volunteers) during a 15-month period commencing in 1995. The mothers formed the cornerstone of a data set of 35 interviewed mothers, 32 interviewed daughters, and 22 interviewed caregivers. GSBB mothers were defined as women who were admitted to GSBB and who attended at least one meeting. Both current and former members were interviewed. The data provide a profile of the girls, their lives, their relationships with their mothers and caregivers, their response to their mothers' incarceration, and their experience with the Girl Scouts.

4. A modified Hudson Parent-Child Contentment Scale [Hudson 1982] is a standardized measure of a parent's and a child's self-reported feelings about one another, gauging liking, trusting, enjoying, understanding, valuing, and supporting one another. The Piers-Harris Children's Self-Concept Scale [Piers 1984] is a self-report measure of a girl's self-concept, viewing the global self-concept, and six dimensions of the self-

concept. The Conners' Parent Rating Scale [Conners 1990] is a standardized measure of five categories of possible problem behavior patterns of children: conduct problems, learning problems, psychosomatic problems, impulsive-hyperactive behavior problems, and anxiety. Fessler's Worry Scale [Fessler 1991] is a self-report measure of the extent to which inmate mothers worry about their child's life situation, feelings, and reunification.

References

Adalist-Estrin, A. (1994). Children of incarcerated parents. *Family and Corrections Network Report 3*, 1–2.

Baunach, P. J. (1982). You can't be a mother and be in prison...Can you? In B. Price & N. Sokoloff (Eds.), *The criminal justice system and women*. New York: Boardman.

Baunach, P. J. (1985). *Mothers in prison*. New Brunswick, NJ: Transaction Books.

Beatty, C. (1997). *Parents in prison: Children in crisis*. Washington, DC: CWLA Press.

Bloom, B., & Steinhart, D. (1993). *Why punish the children: A reappraisal*. San Francisco: National Council on Crime and Delinquency.

Chesney-Lind, M. (1992). Putting the brakes on the building binge. *Corrections Today, 54*, 6, 30, 32–34.

Clark, J. (1995). The impact of the prison environment on mothers. *The Prison Journal, 75*, 306–329.

Clement, M. J. (1993). Parenting in prison: A national survey of programs for incarcerated women. *Journal of Offender Rehabilitation, 19*(1/2), 89–100.

Conners, K. C. (1990). *Conners' Rating Scales Manual*. New York: Multi-Health Systems, Inc.

Datesman, S. K., & Cales, G. L. (1983). "I'm still the same mommy": Maintaining the mother/child relationship in prison. *Prison Journal, 63*(2), 142–154.

Feinman, C. (1986). *Women in the criminal justice system*. New York: Praeger Publisher.

Fessler, S. R. (1991) *Mothers in the correctional system: Separation from children and reunification after incarceration*. Albany, NY: State University of New York (doctoral dissertation).

Fritsch, T. A., & Burkhead, J. D. (1982). Behavioral reactions of children to parental absence due to imprisonment. *Family Relations, 30*(1), 83–88.

Fuller, L. G. (1993). Visitors to women's prisons in California: An exploratory study. *Federal Probation, 57*(4), 41–47.

Gabel, S. (1992). Children of incarcerated and criminal parents: Adjustment, behavior, and prognosis. *Bulletin of American Academy of Psychiatry Law, 20*(1), 33–45.

Gilliard, D. K., & Beck, A. J. (1998). *Bureau of Justice Statistics bulletin: Prison and jail inmates at midyear 1997.* Washington, DC: U.S. Department of Justice, Bureau of Justice Statistics.

Grossman, J. (1984). *Female commitments 1982: The family.* Report prepared for the New York Department of Correctional Services.

Hadley, J. (1981). *Georgia women prison inmates and their families.* Atlanta, GA: Emory University (Master's thesis).

Hairston, C. F., & Lockett, D. (1985). Parents in prison. *Child Abuse and Neglect, 9,* 471–477.

Henriques, Z. W. (1982). *Imprisoned mothers and their children: A descriptive and analytic study.* Washington, DC: University Press of America.

Hudson, W. (1982). *The clinical measurement package: A field manual.* Chicago: Dorsey.

Hungerford, G. P. (1993). *The children of inmate mothers: An exploratory study of children, caregivers and inmate mothers in Ohio* (Ohio State University, doctoral dissertation).

Johnston, D. (1995). The care and placement of prisoners' children. In K. Gabel & D. Johnston (Eds.), *Children of incarcerated parents* (pp. 103–123). New York: Lexington Books.

Johnston, D. (1994). What we know about children of offenders. *Family and Corrections Network Report, 3,* 3–4.

Johnston, D., & Gabel, K. (1995). Incarcerated parents. In K. Gabel & D. Johnston (Eds.), *Children of incarcerated parents* (pp. 3–20). New York: Lexington Books.

Kiser, G. C. (1991). Female inmates and their families. *Federal Probation, 55*(1), 56–63.

LeFlore, L., & Holston, M. A. (1989). Perceived importance of parenting behaviors as reported by inmate mothers: An exploratory study. *Journal of Offender Counseling Services and Rehabilitation, 14*(1), 5–21.

Logan, G. (1992). Family ties take top priority in women's visiting program. *Corrections Today, 54*(6), 160–161.

McGowan, B., & Blumenthal, K. (1978). *Why punish the children? A study of children of women prisoners.* Hackensack, NJ: National Council of Crime and Delinquency.

Moses, M. (1995). Keeping incarcerated mothers and their daughters together: Girl Scouts Beyond Bars. *National Institute of Justice Program Focus.* Washington, DC: U.S. Department of Justice.

Mumola, C. J., & Beck, A. J. (1997). *Prisoners in 1996.* Washington, DC: U.S. Department of Justice, Bureau of Justice Statistics.

Neto, V. V., & Bainer, L. M. (1983). Mother and wife locked up—A day with the family. *The Prison Journal, 63,* 125–141.

Piers, E. V. (1984). *Piers-Harris Children's Self-Concept Scale: Revised Manual 1984.* Los Angeles: Western Psychological Services.

Radish, K. (1994, November 6). Mothers behind bars: The pain of separation never goes away. *The Milwaukee Journal,* pp. 11–15.

Rocheleau, A. M. (1987). *Joining incarcerated mothers with their children: Evaluation of the Lancaster Visiting Cottage Program.* Boston: Massachusetts Department of Corrections.

Simon, R. J., & Landis, J. (1991). *The crimes women commit: The punishments they receive.* Lexington, MA: Lexington Books.

Stanton, S. (1980). *When mothers go to jail.* Boston, MA: D. C. Heath.

Task Force on Youth Development and Community Programs. (1992). *A matter of time: Risk and opportunity in the nonschool hours.* New York: Carnegie Corporation of New York, Carnegie Council on Adolescent Development.

Zalba, S. (1964). *Women prisoners and their families.* CA: Delmar Publishers.

Earning Trust from Youths
6 with None to Spare

Marsha Weissman and Candace Mayer LaRue

The Center for Community Alternatives (CCA) operates an array of programs that primarily serve students whose parents are incarcerated. The authors explore outreach and programmatic approaches and discuss the benefits of a holistic, multifaceted, open approach to identifying, assessing, and meeting the needs of adolescent children of incarcerated parents. The article concludes with policy recommendations regarding further development of programs targeting this population.

Marsha Weissman, M.P.A., is Executive Director; and Candace Mayer LaRue, B.A., is Director of Training and Community Resources, Center for Community Alternatives, Syracuse, NY.

T he incarceration of parents has a particularly devastating impact upon the children left behind. Children of incarcerated parents experience a range of emotions regarding the loss of their parent, complicated by family, school, and community circumstances. With more than 1.7 million people currently incarcerated in jail or prison [Gilliard & Beck 1998] and a total of 5.4 million adults under some form of correctional supervision, there may be as many as 10 million minor children of criminal offenders [Johnston & Carlin 1996]. This number includes children whose parents are presently incarcerated as well as those whose parents were incarcerated at some time in the recent past. Too often, the special needs of these children go unaddressed; further, the social stigma attached to incarceration encourages both children and families to conceal the problem. Given the size of this population, professionals in all fields are likely to encounter children of prisoners regularly [Johnston 1993], and schools, social service, and mental health programs all need to develop programs that are responsive to the needs of these children.

This article explores one program's outreach efforts and programmatic approaches that have encouraged youths ages 12 to 16 enrolled in alternative programs at the middle and high school levels to self-identify and to participate in support groups for children of incarcerated parents or to participate in such groups following identification by school and program staff.

Effects on Adolescents of Parental Incarceration

Children of incarcerated parents have long been referred to as a "hidden population" [Rosenkrantz & Joshua 1982]. The stigma of parental incarceration makes identification of this group of youths difficult. Family deception and secrecy contribute to the difficulty in identifying children of incarcerated parents. Children may be deceived about their parent's incarceration or, even when informed, may be directed by their caregivers to maintain secrecy [Sack et al. 1976]. Such secrecy is often prompted by real or perceived threats to the family's well-being [Chaney et al. 1977]. Children of incarcerated parents are often transient, because their families may frequently move due to economic circumstances [Sack et al. 1976] or because they are transferred from one caregiver to another [McGowan & Blumenthal 1978; Woodrow 1992]. Such instability tends to keep them from settling down long enough to form the necessary level of trust to ask for help [Sack et al. 1976; Dressel & Barnhill 1991]. Frequent moves create an additional obstacle to working with these youths, because the youths may not remain in a program setting long enough to be engaged in services. Each of these issues compounds the secrecy that surrounds parental incarceration and increases the difficulties encountered in identifying, assessing, and meeting the needs of these youths.

Social stigmatization experienced by children of incarcerated parents contributes to a range of reactions on the part of these children. Fritsch and Burkhead [1981] found the children's reactions differed by the gender of the incarcerated parent: "acting out" behavior (i.e., running away or truancy) was associated with paternal incarceration and "acting in" behavior (i.e., crying, withdrawal) was associated with maternal incarceration. Deception regarding parental imprisonment has been associated with delinquency, aggression, and other negative behavior insofar as it prevents children from working through their feelings [Gabel 1992; Hannon et al. 1984]. Deception has also been found to contribute to increased fears and mistrust among children [Hermann-Keeling 1988].

Program Model: Description and Context

The Youth Advocacy Program

The Youth Advocacy Program (YAP) is one of several programs operated by the Center for Community Alternatives (CCA), a private, not-for-profit organization that develops and promotes community-based alternatives to incarceration. CCA operates several programs through offices in Syracuse, New York, and New York City. The Syracuse-based YAP offers a range of advocacy, support, and youth development opportunities for high-risk youths between the ages of 12 and 17 involved in the juvenile justice system and who attend the alternative schools in the Syracuse City School District.

Upon entry into CCA youth programs, students are assessed through a screening process that includes a questionnaire and a brief interview with a staff member. At that time, students are specifically asked about a variety of stress factors that may be present in their lives, including parental incarceration. Assessment is an ongoing process, as additional information is often revealed through program participation. Youths are offered access to a variety of programs that meet their specific needs upon initial assessment, and again as other needs arise or become apparent. Such services may include mentoring, participation in a peer education program, classroom sessions, or job training.

A critical element of the service design is encouraging youths to participate in more than one YAP project. To that end, service referrals are frequently made directly to other CCA programs, including CHOICES, an HIV/AIDS prevention, education, and peer leadership training program; Self-Development, a work apprenticeship program; JUMP, a juvenile mentoring program; and Community Corps, a community service-learning program. Youth Advocacy also provides case planning, court advocacy, and community supervision for youths in the juvenile justice system, as an alternative to placement. YAP is staffed by a Director of Youth Services and has one or more staff specialists assigned to each individual project. YAP also has access to resources through other CCA programs, including a substance abuse evaluator and a court advocate. These varied programs share in common a strong, "unconditional" commitment to youths.

This philosophy, along with the variety of program options, promotes trust and credulity among high-risk youths that in turn allows them to feel comfortable in disclosing what otherwise would be a family secret—the incarceration of a parent. CCA developed the Children of Incarcerated Parents (ChIPs) support group as an additional, specific response to the reality that more than 50% of the youths in CCA programs identified themselves during initial screening as having experienced the incarceration of one or both parents, and an additional 30% were subsequently identified during the course of the program year.

Client Characteristics

Youths who participate in YAP services mirror the demographic characteristics of students who attend the Beard Alternative School. New York State Education Department 1994-1995 data show the following characteristics for Beard School students. Two-thirds (67%) of the student population is African American, with 30% Caucasian and the balance other minorities (Latino and American Indian). In contrast, the school district's population as a whole is 53% Caucasian. Performance data from 1995-1996 show a 61% attendance rate in Beard and a 40% dropout rate, compared to a 91% annual attendance rate and 5% dropout rate for the district at large. The school also had an 82% suspension rate compared to a suspension rate of 10% for the district. Eighty-seven percent of the Beard students are eligible for free lunch. Without exception, students in the Beard School tested below students in other Syracuse district schools in all tested subject areas.

In the 1996-97 school year, CCA's YAP programs served 128 youths whose sociodemographic characteristics are as follows: average age of 14.1 years; 64% male, 36% female; and 74% African American, 5% Latino, 5% biracial, 14% Caucasian, 1% American Indian, and 1% Asian. At least 90% of the students come from low-income families and 80% were identified as having had a parent or guardian who has been incarcerated. With regard to the youths' juvenile justice involvement, 78% reported involvement in the juvenile justice system.

Program Approaches to Building Trust

To address the range of youth needs, CCA makes use of diverse funding sources, offers positive opportunities for youths, seeks community support and involvement, and gains adult participation and commitment as mentors, job supervisors, and community supervisors. The program design also took into consideration several key factors related to outreach and recruitment, staffing, and program philosophy and purposes. YAP programs use an open approach to intake. There are no *a priori* exclusionary criteria: youths are generally welcome to participate in YAP programs regardless of school, social service, or criminal justice system history.

Considerable effort is made by staff members to establish rapport with the youths. This requires attention to methods of outreach and staffing. As CCA programs are co-located in the Beard School, they are directly on site and available to the youths every school day. Youths are encouraged to come into CCA's office and some program activities are scheduled in that setting.

In designing the CCA programs, it was important to adapt the program settings so as to make them accessible, attractive and responsive to an inner city, minority, youthful population. The office environment is conducive to visits by the youths and contributes to building bonds between youths and program staff. All CCA staff, whether direct program or other, have been trained to be friendly and attentive to youths and office support staff soon come to know the youths by name. Also attracting the youths is an office decor that reflects a multicultural client group, with information and posters reflective of aspects of African American and Latino culture and brochures and information available in Spanish and English. YAP has food and drink available for its youths, recognizing that teenagers are often hungry.

Building trust and rapport also requires attentiveness to staffing considerations, specifically cultural competence. The multiethnic YAP team includes African Americans, Latinos, and Caucasians. The staff has generally been balanced between men and women. Two of the staff who work with the support group were themselves children of incarcerated parents, and are willing to discuss that fact with youths in the ChIPs program.

Youths are referred to CCA by school staff, law guardians,[1] and peers, and by self-referral. In addition, the Beard School has integrated CCA's Community Corps service-learning program directly into the school curriculum and all seventh and ninth graders must participate in this class. All youths entering CCA programs undergo a comprehensive psychosocial assessment of their individual and family circumstances. In addition to interviewing the youths, program staff members interview parents and review school and juvenile justice records.

The assessment is regarded as the first opportunity to establish rapport with the youths. It also provides an opportunity for staff to learn of the incarceration of a parent. Because the question of parental incarceration is included in the assessment as one of many difficult questions, and because staff actually take the time to ask the question, more than half of the youths who have an incarcerated parent identify themselves during the initial assessment interview. During the assessment, the staff also present information to the youths about CCA's programs and purposes and offer assistance in addressing parental needs.

For reasons identified earlier, however, at least half of the youths are reluctant to discuss their parent's incarceration and their own juvenile justice involvement. The assessment process is, by design, considered to be an ongoing, collaborative process. Staff meet regularly to discuss individual students. Networking with the community centers that also serve the youths takes place on an informal basis; additional efforts are underway through a federally funded juvenile gun violence prevention initiative to create a more formal system of integrated case management.

Finally, CCA's program design recognizes that youths and

their families are likely to respond in a variety of ways to what may be perceived as power and authority in service delivery. Program staff expect their credibility to be tested and challenged. Continuing to reach out to youths in the face of these challenges is critical to earning trust among youths who have little to spare.

ChIPS Support: Meeting the Needs of Adolescent Children of Incarcerated Parents

Program assessment practices and the program options that build trust and meet a wide variety of needs enabled CCA to determine that 80% of the youths enrolled in CCA programs have a parent who is presently or was recently incarcerated. Despite the prevalence of parental incarceration, there were no services available in the Syracuse area that specifically addressed issues of parental incarceration. Previous programs, including a program to help families visit inmates incarcerated in distant state prisons and a program to help maintain ties between women incarcerated in the local jail facility and their children, are defunct due to loss of funding.

With support from a local foundation (the MONY Foundation) and the cooperation of the Syracuse City School District, CCA established psychoeducational support groups for children of incarcerated parents. CCA's experience in recruiting youths to participate in these groups underscores the obstacles created by the social stigma and family deception surrounding this issue. Despite an awareness that 80% of youths served by CCA were children of incarcerated parents, initial support group recruitment efforts were unsuccessful. Posters placed throughout the building and staff presentations to classes resulted in the referral or self-identification of only 10 students. Furthermore, efforts to enlist parent support and interest by initially requiring parental permission to participate resulted in delays and contributed to poor results during early recruitment efforts. Only one of the first

10 parents contacted returned the permission form; in several instances the letters were returned as undeliverable. Two caregivers refused to allow students to participate. In one case, the student reported that her aunt refused permission because she did not want anyone involved in their "personal" business; in the other, the previously incarcerated father stated that he wanted to get on with life, denying the child's problems.

To counter these obstacles, a new strategy was developed based upon the practices currently in place in the school system for other support groups.[2] In the redesign of ChIPs, parental permission was no longer required, although no student whose parent objected to the program was permitted to attend. New posters were designed that highlighted the availability of food at the groups. Students were recruited through direct presentations to CCA's Learn and Serve classes; these students were also asked to encourage their friends to attend. Guidance counselors and social workers at the school continued to serve as referral sources, and teachers directly referred children in younger grades.

ChIPS offered three support groups at the Beard School during the spring of 1997, with up to 10 youths in each group, and an open enrollment process that allowed students to enter at any point in the group. One group was all seventh grade boys, one was all seventh grade girls, and the third was a mixed gender group of younger students. The girls' group continued during the summer.

Curriculum Materials

ChIPS presently uses a curriculum under development by CCA that covers issues of isolation, self-esteem, and shame; helps children to develop ways to deal with other children and adults regarding their absent parent; helps youths to make positive choices, set goals, and develop support systems; addresses substance abuse; and promotes an understanding of the corrections system (visiting, contact, parole, release) and legal issues. The support groups are psychoeducational in nature. Each session is developed through an interactive process, which typically begins with informal discussion during a shared lunch. As the youths talk about issues of immediate importance, the facilitators use the curriculum manual as a resource to steer the discussion in a solution-focused manner. For example, if a group member shared concerns about a parent who had been arrested recently, a section in the manual on "Understanding the Criminal Justice System" would help address both specific factual issues such as visiting guidelines at the local facility and empowerment issues such as learning how to research one's own specific questions about a parent's case. In response to shame and stigma as ongoing issues, the manual could be used to help educate the youths about the prevalence of parental incarceration both from a larger statistical point of view and from the context of the numbers of youths enrolled in a particular school. Discussion about the effects of racism on incarceration rates in the neighborhoods where the youths reside is also encouraged, with a focus on finding positive solutions both as individuals and as members of the community. To this end, youths who are not already enrolled in CCA programs are encouraged to participate in the other programs offered by the agency. These other programs allow ChIPs students a range of positive opportunities, and provide adult support and recognition. Where CCA programs cannot meet youths' needs, referrals are made to appropriate services such as psychological counseling.

Group Formation

Experiences during the program's first year resulted in the current establishment of two support groups, with a third group due to be added soon. Middle-school age girls and boys participate in gender-specific groups. The groups meet weekly in a classroom located in an isolated wing of the school that allows for a reasonable degree of privacy for the students. The sessions are scheduled during a combined lunch and physical education time slot, allowing for an hour-long session. A mixed-gender group is no longer offered because the facilitators found that when boys and girls were in the support group together, there tended to be more game playing and less focused discussion.

The current groups are limited in enrollment to a maximum of eight youths, with enrollment accepted only during the first few sessions, or upon consultation with the group. Having more than eight youths, it was found, made it difficult for individuals to speak openly about the situations in their lives. In addition, once the students developed a sense of trust and safety with each other, it became too disruptive to the dynamics of the group to allow new students to join. Since in some cases a new student might be an integrated part of the peer group, however, new members may be added with the permission of the existing group members.

Despite the students' familiarity with and trust in CCA staff due to previous associations, most of the first sessions with each group are spent reassuring the students that the sessions will remain confidential. Students in each group have expressed a strong desire to ensure that no one outside the group learn the specifics of their family situations. Staff have noticed this desire for confidentiality to carry over into other programs, with youths being very careful in casual conversations to avoid revealing the nature of the support group.

An important aspect of the groups' initial sessions is the development of safety in the group. To create a safe environment, great care is taken in staffing, and in the development and enforcement of ground rules. The groups are each cofacilitated by members of the youth staff, with careful attention to matching appropriate staff members to the groups. The facilitation teams are racially diverse and are matched to the groups by gender. In each case, at least one of the team members was also the child of an incarcerated parent during his or her lifetime. During the initial sessions, the groups generate a list of ground rules for themselves, with guidance from the facilitators. All groups are expected to agree to basic rules including: confidentiality; no "put-downs"; one person speaks at a time; speaking from one's own experience only; and having the right to pass. These basic rules are not given out in a list, but rather are developed through a brainstorming discussion by the group. For example, this year's group of girls added "no cussing" and "stay seated if you are angry" to the list for their group.

Discussions during the sessions have focused on a range of issues, including multiple placements, juvenile delinquency among the students and their siblings, and high levels of family violence. Every student in the program has expressed relief at being able to talk about parental incarceration; for those teens who witnessed their parents' arrest, ChIPs has generally been the first time they were able to express the feelings of fear, grief, and anger that they experienced during that traumatic event.

The Trust Building Process: Case Examples

Carmen

Carmen[3] is a 13-year-old female who has had multiple out-of-home placements, including several stays at the local juvenile detention facility. She was a latecomer to the group, entering after the group had already met several times. The first time she came to the support group, she exhibited a lack of trust so strong that she refused to taste the pizza being shared for lunch because she did not eat food from unfamiliar restaurants. The facilitators expressed concern about the fact that she would not have an opportunity to eat lunch and asked her to let them know which sorts of food she was willing to eat so that future meals could take her needs into account. Great care was taken by the facilitators to ensure that Carmen felt included, and the group welcomed her by briefly sharing their names, and their opinions of the group. As the session progressed and Carmen's primary needs were addressed, she became visibly more comfortable. Within an hour, she had not only eaten the pizza, but had also shared specific details of a current court case for which she needed assistance.

Tyrone

Youths in the support groups frequently do not know where their fathers are located and/or the specifics of the crime committed by their parents. An extreme case is that of Tyrone, whose father had been incarcerated since he was very young. Tyrone had always assumed that his sister's death was the reason for the incarceration, and only learned in the group, from his brother who was also participating, that this was not the case. Although it is unusual for the information about a missing parent to be so readily available, it is not unusual to find that once the student has indicated a desire to know more about the circumstances of the missing parent, it becomes easier for the youth to also ask for information from family and friends, sometimes with the aid of a CCA staff member.

Kirsten

Kirsten had been present when her mother was arrested on drug charges. Appearing considerably older than 14, Kirsten was also detained briefly in the local jail. Released to her grandmother, she was not allowed to discuss the experience, and was also discouraged from talking about it when her mother was released. Months later, during a ChIPs meeting, she described the arrest in excruciating detail, actually jumping out of her chair to act out some of the actions that the police had taken. At the end of her story, she sat back in her chair and thanked the facilitator who was present for the session, stating that this was her first opportunity to tell her story.

Conclusion

Meeting the needs of children of incarcerated parents requires a multifaceted, collaborative approach. Using information available from program and school staff, networking across agencies, and providing tangible benefits (pizza, field trips) are all necessary tactics for breaking through the wall of secrecy that isolates these children and their families. Strong community advocacy and standing up for and with children and their families in courts, schools, and government and community agencies are key to building the trust necessary to address the myriad issues facing children of incarcerated parents.

Schools and community programs need to develop creative and flexible approaches to working with these children. A first step in identifying children of incarcerated parents is to include questions regarding parental incarceration in all assessment tools, recognizing that youths with incarcerated parents are the very same ones who present themselves at alternative schools and other secondary prevention and intervention programs designed for youths at risk. Using existing youth development services as a starting point (mentoring, job training, peer educator programs) has proven to be a mechanism for developing trust among youths sufficient to allow them to then disclose the specifics of their family situations. Programs must stress confidentiality to provide the safety needed for meaningful dialogue in the groups.

New efforts at working with the children's current caregivers are underway at CCA, using the same model that worked with the youths. Materials are in the development stages to assist the caregivers in understanding the special needs of children of incarcerated parents. Parents will be contacted first under the auspices of CCA's other programs, with discussion of parental incarceration introduced once the relationship between the agency and the caregiver has developed into one of trust. ◆

Notes

1. In New York State, persons convicted of felony-level offenses and sentenced to more than one year of incarceration must serve their sentences in state correctional facilities. All misdemeanor sentences and felony sentences of one year or less are served in local facilities.

2. For example, the school district sponsors a support group, "Banana Splits," for children of divorced, separated, or otherwise fragmented families. Students can participate in this group without parental permission and information disclosed in the group is deemed confidential.

3. The examples have been changed slightly to disguise participants' identities.

References

Chaney, R., Linkenhoker, D., & Horne, A. (1977). The counselor and children of imprisoned parents. *Elementary School Guidance and Counseling, 11,* 177–183.

Dressel, P. L., & Barnhill, S. K. (1991). *Three generations at risk: A model intergenerational program for families of imprisoned mothers.* Atlanta, GA: Aid to Imprisoned Mothers.

Fritsch, T. A., & Burkhead, J. D. (1981, January). Behavioral reactions of children to parental absence due to imprisonment. *Family Relations,* 83–88.

Gabel, S. (1992). Children of incarcerated and criminal parents: Adjustment, behavior, and prognosis. *Bulletin of the American Academy of Psychiatry and the Law, 20,* 33–45.

Gilliard, D. K., & Beck, A. J. (1998). *Bureau of Justice Statistics bulletin: Prison and jail inmates at midyear 1997.* Washington, DC: U.S. Department of Justice, Bureau of Justice Statistics.

Hannon, G., Martin, D., & Martin, M. (1984). Incarceration in the family: Adjustment to change. *Family Therapy, 11,* 253–60

Hermann-Keeling, E. (1988). When dad goes to prison. *Nurturing Today, 10*(15).

Johnston, D. (1993). *Report no. 13: Effects of parental incarceration.* Pasadena, CA: Pacific Oaks Center for Children of Incarcerated Parents.

Johnston, D., & Carlin, M. (1996). Enduring trauma among children of criminal offenders. *Progress: Family Systems Research and Therapy, 5*, 9–36.

McGowan, B. G., & Blumenthal, K. L. (1978). *Why punish the children?* Hackensack, NJ: National Council on Crime & Delinquency.

Rosenkrantz, L., & Joshua, V. (1982, January-February). Children of incarcerated parents: a hidden population. *Children Today*, 2–6.

Sack, W. H., Seidler, T., & Thomas, S. (1976). Children of imprisoned parents: A psychosocial exploration. *American Journal of Orthopsychiatry, 46*, 618–628.

Woodrow, J. (1992). Mothers inside, children outside: What happens to the dependent children of female inmates. In R. Shaw (Ed.), *Prisoners' children: What are the issues?* (pp. 28–39). New York: Routledge.

U. S. Department of Justice. (1995). *Correctional populations in the United States.* Washington, DC: U. S. Department of Justice, Bureau of Justice Statistics.

Developing Quality Services for Offenders and Families: An Innovative Partnership

7

Toni Johnson, Katherine Selber, and Michael Lauderdale

Incarceration and the failures associated with the prison experience—particularly high rates of recidivism—are creating an underclass of men and a cycle of disrupted family relations that represent a worrisome community problem. This article reports on a successful effort to develop a set of services for ex-offenders and their children and families that enhance community integration, to build support networks, and to assist community institutions in mobilizing services for this population. Program components, the development of the program through a school of social work, and illustrations of innovative program activities are highlighted.

Toni Johnson, LMSW, is Field Specialist, School of Social Work, University of Texas at Austin, Austin, TX. Katherine Selber, Ph.D., is Assistant Professor, Department of Social Work, Southwest Texas State University, San Marcos, TX. Michael Lauderdale, Ph.D., is Clara Pope Willoughby Centennial Professor of Social Work, School of Social Work, University of Texas at Austin, Austin, TX.

I ndividual conduct is shaped by the norms and values that are communicated by one's family and neighborhood. To a great extent, crime occurs when family and neighborhood structures fail to impart norms of appropriate conduct to individuals [Lynch 1995]. Social networks, however, can foster positive changes in values and behaviors. Such networks continuously affirm these positive changes through support, vigilance, and consistency. Whether provided by families, corporations, or therapeutic communities, the impact of social networks on behavior is well-established [Garbarino 1982].

Nowhere is the difficulty in establishing or maintaining socially relevant behavior more apparent than in the criminal justice field, and of all criminal justice efforts, none is more challenging than reducing the high rates of recidivism of released offenders that eventuate in reincarcerations. These high recidivism rates suggest that imprisonment itself does not deter future crime and may sometimes contribute to it [Ekland-Ohlson & Kelly 1993; Hairston 1988]. While typical interventions focus upon the offender, substantial theoretical and empirical reasons argue for an examination of interventions that stress social networks that are inclusive of the offender—such as those that focus on the family and the community as social networks.

Systematic work through social networks with families and children as well as communities of offenders has only recently begun to emerge in the criminal justice field as a possible rehabilitation alternative [Adalist-Estrin 1994; Gendreau 1996]. Intervention through natural support systems for offenders is supportable in terms of practical and humanitarian reasons, as well as in terms of the potential for developing positive behaviors in the family system. These networks can help develop a comprehensive social fabric that supports families with multiple needs, especially those with children. Using such supports can lower rates of recidivism, prevent intergenerational patterns of incarceration and, ultimately, lower costs to taxpayers [Hairston 1988].

Interventions in preventing ex-offenders from engaging in criminal activities remain difficult to evaluate [Gendreau 1994], particularly those interventions that offer rehabilitative, community-based approaches outside of the mainstream incarceration approach. Strategies such as community-based programs that provide support to families as well as offenders are an example of an alternative effort. Such alternatives are less costly than traditional approaches and hold the potential of prevention. Moreover, the reality for almost every incarcerated offender is that some of that person's life will be spent outside of prison.

No society can afford the costs of maintaining as large a percentage of its population in prison as has been the trend in the United States in the last decade. In this country, 1.7 million adults are incarcerated in prisons and jails, impacting approximately 1.5 million children who are left behind [Gilliard & Beck 1998].

If community-based programs are to become a recognized alternative, research on their development and effectiveness is needed. This article reports on the development and provision of a community-based program, the Family Support Program for Ex-Offenders (FSP), for working with families and ex-offenders. The project was initially funded in 1992 as part of an innovative partnership by the Texas prison system and the University of Texas at Austin School of Social Work. The program has several unique features that promote quality services to a variety of consumers and stakeholders, including ex-offenders, families and children, the community network of organizations and professionals working in the criminal justice field, and policymakers.

Theoretical Considerations

The developmental and enduring consequence of the immediate social situation upon human behavior is well established throughout the behavioral and social science literature [Sherif & Sherif 1965; McKay 1972; Phillips et al. 1974]. More recently, Blau and

Blau [1982] and Stark [1987] have related deviant or criminal behavior at the level of the individual and small group to the larger
social and cultural contexts.

Understanding the impact of the environment and the
person's fit within family, group, and community systems is of
particular use in addressing various client needs through work
with multiple systems [Whittaker & Garbarino 1983]. Within this
framework, the concept of social support has emerged. *Social support* has been defined in various ways, including mutual aid, assistance, guidance, and feedback either given or inferred
[Whittaker et al. 1986]. In a review of the social support literature, Streeter and Franklin [1992] suggest that social support is a
complex concept with many dimensions including different types
and sources of support. They suggest that such concepts as the
quality of the person's social network, the person's perceived
connectedness to friends and family, and the actual aid given are
all forms of social support. Social support can occur within "natural helping networks" such as friends and family, in mutual aid
or self-help groups, and in formal networks such as with helping
professionals [Whittaker et al. 1986].

The concept of social support has great utility in terms of assessment and intervention for at-risk groups. The presence of
social support helps protect the individual during crises from a
variety of stressful stimuli and can be useful in assisting persons
suffering from illness, unemployment, and other losses [Kaplan
et al. 1977]. In addition, within the juvenile justice field, studies
suggest that the presence of support is a better predictor of outcome than the juvenile's condition at discharge or the severity of
problems at the time of treatment [Whittaker et al. 1986].

As applied to the adult criminal justice field, the social support framework suggests that work at the family and community levels may help mitigate the effects of the prison institution
while supporting the offender and family through the transition
to community living [Ekland-Ohlson et al. 1983; Hannon et al.

1984]. This framework proposes that such support facilitates adjustment and provides help for the offender in dealing with the social and emotional difficulties of incarceration and transition. In addition, social support can assist the prisoner by providing concrete aid in terms of money, clothing, and information about the outside world [Homer 1979]. Moreover, this support provides the inmate with a buffer in living through the prison experience as well as in making the transition to the community. Finally, the framework proposes that the absence of natural support networks can have negative consequences for postrelease behavior. With few or no support networks, the offender faces considerable difficulty in establishing and maintaining appropriate behaviors to remain out of prison once released to the community.

Related Research in Criminal Justice

The application of these conceptual frameworks has had scant utilization within criminal justice. Indeed, the field of corrections has primarily focused its attention on inmate data (especially the individual inmate) and not on information about relationships outside of the prison environment such as those with families and communities [Bloom 1995; Johnston 1995]. Likewise, the family studies field has not emphasized the collection of significant scientific data about families of offenders [Adalist-Estrin 1994; Hairston 1988]. It is not surprising, then, to discover that there is little in the criminal justice literature on the impact of enhancing social support through work with families and children as well as communities.

In terms of enhancing family systems, studies suggest that an inmate's contact (as measured by number of family visits, written correspondence, and participation in furlough programs) with family and friends while still in prison may be important in decreasing recidivism rates and fostering positive behaviors [Adams & Fischer 1976; Holt & Miller 1972; Hostetter & Jinnah

1993; Howser & McDonald 1972; Leclair 1978]. Although few empirical studies exist, the above efforts suggest the need for further exploration of the value of maintaining family ties while in prison. Such contact has clear value as well for the spouse and children of the offender. The reality of the American system of dealing with crimes through incarceration is that it spreads punishment to innocent parties (i.e., the family). Contact during incarceration serves to mitigate some of this punishment.

Family Support Program Services: An Overview

During the past decade, a perplexing revolving door has formed in the Texas prison system. Less serious offenders are entering prison at a higher rate, while more serious offenders, already in prison, are leaving by the "back door" to "make room" for new inmates and ease prison overcrowding. Within this context, the Texas Department of Corrections approached the authors for assistance in developing the Family Support Program (FSP), a community-based rehabilitation effort for offenders, their families and children, and the community.

FSP has now been in operation for five years. Four features of the program make it uniquely suited to providing supportive services: a dual focus on the offender and the family system; a special attention to work with children of offenders; a focus on the community service network; and an emphasis on dynamic predictors of offender reintegration within a community-based format. A number of other innovative features also sets the program apart and provides a transportable model for technology transfer.

Focus on the Offender and the Family System

FSP services concentrate not only on the offender but also on the family system, using a comprehensive case management approach. The family system is defined as any relative or significant other with whom the offender is living or who the offender identifies as being part of his/her family network. Services are short-term and are provided over a three- to nine-month period. Work with the family may begin as early as the prerelease phase or well after the release date of the offender. Early program efforts attempted to work only with those offenders who were 90 days away from release and their families. This entailed linking with case workers in the prisons that promoted FSP services to inmates. This strategy was supplemented in FSP's second year with more families being referred after the offender's release, providing the program with an opportunity to expand the number of clients served. Case finding also includes involvement with parole officers to review potential cases, which may follow a nonroutine path to the program.

Traditional and nontraditional services are part of the service design strategy for the family. Because offenders and their families are often reluctant to come to traditional service agencies, the FSP effort has aggressively sought to involve clients in services. For example, approximately 75% of individual services are delivered within the home in order to increase client participation and success.

Individual and family services include supportive and educational counseling with the offender only, the family only, or the offender and the family together. A psychosocial assessment is completed with both the family and the offender, stressing the comprehensive needs of the client system (legal, economic, housing, medical, psychological, health, transportation, employment, and social). A service plan is then developed and monitored throughout the remainder of the client's involvement in services. Case management services also include routine meetings and coordination with a variety of parole department staff, including parole officers and administrative staff.

Group services are broad based and include both offenders and family members. These services are designed with a dual

focus: (1) to enhance the offender's reintegration through providing information, support, and education for successful coping and problem-solving skills; and (2) to assist family members
in their coping and development. A variety of group services for
offenders and adult family members has been offered, including
a support group for ex-offenders and their families; a support
group for the male residents of a halfway house; an anger management group for male parolees; support groups for caregivers;
drop-in groups for parolees; a family support group for wives,
girlfriends, and mothers; and a female offenders support group.
Groups have been designed as primarily ongoing in nature and
meet once a week. Most group services have been offered within
other community settings to increase family involvement and participation. Part of the service design is to make it difficult for offenders and families to avoid the services. Thus, the FSP model
serves to increase the general level of social visibility and control
that the community has with the offender and the family.

To date, FSP has served more than 1,200 family system units
with case management services. Of the offenders served, approximately 86% have been males and 14% females. These figures are
representative of efforts at the case management level and are
not inclusive of all group services.

Focus on Work with Children of Offenders

FSP provides for outreach and both individual and group work
with children of offenders. Individual services are primarily
home-based, with a strong emphasis on information and referral. In addition, since 1995, work with children in school settings
has been at the core of both individual and group services for
children.

In terms of group services for children, 62 children have been
served in groups designed specifically for children of incarcerated parents. Most groups for children have been designed as
support groups, although others have focused on loss, drop-in

recreational services, and socialization. One example of a children's group was a support group organized at a community elementary school for third- to fifth-grade students whose parents had been incarcerated. Of the eight children in this group, six showed improved behavior in class, according to teacher reports. In addition, four had improved attendance, and three had improved grades after participation in the support group.

Counselors and teachers report a variety of improvements from children participating in the groups at the middle-school level. For example, teachers reported that in one support group with five members—three Hispanic and two African Americans—three showed a decrease in referrals for detention and four showed a decrease in class disruptions. Of these five group members, four of the five were self-identified gang members, some from rival gangs. All of these youth remained in the group and were able to forge new friendships that carried over after the group terminated. Such efforts are reflective of the design of FSP, which serves to address behaviors of both the offender and the family.

Recently, group activities with the school-age children have been expanded by two of the School of Social Work's faculty members with expertise in group work. Data are being collected and analyzed from two support groups for elementary school students. The study uses an experimental design and control group to look at improvements in self-esteem as a result of participation in the support groups.

The program's work with children has relied heavily on collaboration with other social service agencies, with FSP staff members facilitating linkages among the criminal justice, child welfare, and social service staffs. For example, a meeting for child welfare, juvenile justice, and criminal justice policymakers was sponsored by FSP to facilitate collaboration and problem solving on crosscutting issues. FSP staff members also provide workshops for regional child protective services staff on strategies and techniques for working with children of incarcerated parents. This training shares the knowledge developed by FSP over the past five years with workers with both in-home and out-of-home placement responsibility.

Focus on the Community Service Network

Community-building services are an important focus of FSP. Enhancing community services for this population has involved a three-pronged approach: (1) developing an active advocacy and referral approach to work with families; (2) building a database of community services and monitoring the relative responsiveness of agencies; and (3) participating in efforts to coordinate all services to offenders and families within one facility.

Advocacy and Referral. FSP staff members make many referrals in behalf of offenders and their family members and work closely with education-related agencies such as skill-training programs for offenders and spouses. Their efforts to target school systems educating children of offenders have resulted in networking with teachers, school counselors, and principals to support the academic, social, and emotional needs of the children. Housing agencies have also been drawn into the network to help with the substantial problems that families face in securing adequate housing. Employment programs, including skills training and job search programs; alcohol and substance abuse services; and health services, including basic clinic and intermediary care, are regularly called upon to provide services to offenders and families.

Other advocacy approaches include presentations to agencies and educational campaigns in behalf of clients to identify and bridge gaps in services. Presentations have been made in the community describing FSP services to local religious organizations, offender advocacy groups, criminal justice organizations, and other human service organizations. International, national, and statewide presentations provide information and training to those professionals who frequently provide services to families of offenders in other settings.

Since offenders and their families are generally not given preference or high priority by many traditional service agencies, advocacy and the building of supportive relationships with service providers have been major focuses of the program. Outreach activities have also included newsletters to families and inmates to disseminate information about services and to maintain contact with client systems.

The magnitude of the need for community network building activities can be understood by examining the number of referrals made for the offenders and families. A 1997 examination of all 200 active cases showed that approximately 7.5 referrals were made on average per offender served. A closer look at types of referrals provides information about planning efforts needed at the macro-level, as well the needs of the offenders and families themselves. Of the referrals made, approximately 24% were for housing-related services, 19% for basic needs such as food and clothing, 15% for health- and disability-related services, 12% for mental health and substance abuse issues, 9% for employment and training services, 7% for child and youth services for family members, 4% for legal services, and 10% for a broad arena of services, including transportation and general neighborhood services. Of the referrals made in this group of 200 cases, approximately 40% were completed (i.e., the clients followed through with services), about 27% did not complete the referrals, and in about 33% of the cases, information about follow-through was incomplete or unavailable.

These data indicate that offenders and families have multiple social service needs, including help in crisis situations, as well as assistance with basic needs. The data also highlight the importance of having interventions focused on teaching families about community services and how to follow through on referrals.

Building a Database. The second approach to community building activities has been the development of the database of community services described by the referrals above. This computerized database, with approximately 384 agencies, assists FSP workers in their case management training and their information and referral activities. Cross-relational searches can be performed by type of referral needed, referrals made for a given client, and general information about the agency and services. This system is the foundation for increased communication, monitoring, and reporting activities. It permits the identification of client needs, facilitates the tracking of client progress, and provides a window on the effectiveness of referrals to any agency.

Coordination. The third approach to community building activities has revolved around a new service design strategy to provide a common facility for organizations that serve the needs of offenders and their families. Such a one-site approach would facilitate access to services for this population. This resource center functions under the parole division's auspices and is a focal point for volunteer recruitment and social service agency involvement. FSP provides staffing coverage for this program and has advocated promoting this approach with policymakers.

Focus on Dynamic Predictors of Offender Reintegration in a Community-Based Format

FSP's philosophy is underscored by a focus on dynamic as opposed to static predictors of recidivism [Gendreau 1994]. Static predictors are those issues rooted in the past that cannot be changed, such as criminal history, family of origin variables, socioeconomic variables, race, and intellectual functioning. These variables have been heavily used by traditional corrections approaches for assessing risk, although they are of varying use in terms of predicting recidivism. Dynamic predictors include such variables as attitudes and beliefs about criminal behavior, education, employment, substance abuse, and interpersonal conflict. They have been found in recent studies to be as good as static factors in predicting recidivism [Gendreau 1994].

The primary difference in the two types of predictors, however, is that dynamic predictors provide an intervention focus for change. For example, FSP staff members complete a psychosocial assessment that includes many of the static predictors mentioned above. Interventions for a "typical case," however, might involve housing assistance, employment training, health clinic cards, involvement in a support group to talk about relationship difficulties in the family and community, monitoring of financial need, and home visits to talk with family. The needs targeted by FSP staff are related to present functioning and tied to the prevention of recidivism only indirectly by building positive behaviors.

In addition, the program is a community-based effort rooted in a noninstitutional approach to service provision. The coupling of these two strategies provides opportunities for working on strengths of family systems as well as a broad lens inclusive of community interventions by the program.

This approach focuses intervention on helping the entire family and community cope with the multiple challenges of criminal behavior, not just on the future recidivism of the offender, as important as this factor is to program success. The challenge for this program, as for most other community-based efforts, is how to measure change along other important indices.

Innovative Features

In addition to the above core program characteristics, FSP makes use of a number of innovations that other schools of social work and agencies interested in developing similar projects should consider. The program is now expanding to a second major metropolitan area within Texas.

The Educational Enterprise Model. The response to the governor's and the state correction agency's request originated within the school's internship office and with the chair holder in criminal justice in the School of Social Work. Originally, the project's design called for a staff of a small team of two M.S.W.s, in conjunction with a field unit of 8-10 bachelor- and master's-level social work interns. This approach addressed the school's training goal and the criminal justice agency's need to develop a pool of qualified personnel in this field.

This field unit is unique because it most closely resembles a freestanding agency such as the university teaching hospital model within the medical profession. Because services to families and children of offenders had not been delivered by the criminal justice system in the past, this project represented an attempt to develop a prototype for service delivery.

In addition, the correctional agency that funded FSP was interested in developing a pool of potential job-ready social workers for employment purposes. This agency interest is of course a good fit with the school's training mission. Using a field practicum as a mechanism for evaluating a potential job applicant is common practice in many field agencies.

To date, the FSP field unit has trained a total of 61 social work students—44 at the bachelor's level and 17 at the master's level. Of these, 69% were Caucasian, 13% were African American, 12% were Latino, and 6% were members of other minorities. A total of 21% have worked in criminal justice settings after graduation.

Another illustration of the training potential of FSP can be found in a follow-up survey of the first cohort of 10 participating interns. Of this group, 51% reported interest in the criminal justice field prior to entering the project for their internship. Of the remaining 49% of interns who did not have prior interest, approximately half (50%) reported having developed an interest in the field at the end of their internship experience [Selber et al. 1993]. These data suggest the potential impact on recruitment from this type of educational endeavor.

Training students to work with families and children of incarcerated parents as well as with offenders has required a special curriculum beyond the core family material offered in the social work program. Additional features of the training include knowledge and skills in the criminal justice system and process; the impact of incarceration on children and families; dynamics of poverty, single parenthood, substance abuse, and multineed families typical of this population; collaborative teamwork and interdisciplinary work; parent training; safety issues; and advocacy and community networking. Social work students in FSP have also been challenged by the importance of prioritizing the basic needs of children and families. Understanding and implementing strategies to address the multitude of basic family needs require a focus on essential social work skills rather than highly clinical therapeutic skills.

FSP has also been a particularly rich source of curriculum innovations for the school of social work, as seen in the field internship seminar (which focuses on the specific client population relevant to the field unit) and in other areas of the school's curriculum. Elective courses are a good example of the impact of the project on the rest of the curriculum. For example, the lower division course on criminal justice has drawn on the experiences from FSP through the use of guest speakers from the networks of professionals created by the program.

Mandate for Innovations in Service Delivery. From the correctional agency's perspective, the essence of the project continues to be the partnership for assisting the agency in developing innovative services. The benchmarking of quality services is a private sector trend now affecting the human services field [Lauderdale 1998a, 1998b; Martin 1993; Selber 1998]. This model of program development provides a mechanism for benchmarking, with an emphasis on cross-system and interdisciplinary collaboration and on developing quality services by using an educational enterprise to develop new service strategies. Development of quality services requires a commitment to research and data collection that can be best supported when a university is closely involved in program development.

The Advisory Council: A Mechanism for Ongoing Partnership. One of the most important components of FSP has been the Advisory Council, which provides ongoing guidance and input into program development, procedure, and policy formulation, as well as evaluation. The Advisory Council comprises members of the School of Social Work, the contracting/host agency, other key agencies that serve the same client population, funding agency representatives, and consumer groups. Other agencies with overlapping client systems are also represented. It is worth noting that this project reflects a unique collaboration between the institutional division and parole departments of the criminal justice system. Historically, these components of the criminal justice system in Texas have struggled over philosophical issues and priorities within their own system.

Preliminary Program Results

Two studies have been completed on recidivism results of the program. Data on recidivism are reported as one measure of "success" at this time since the processing of other outcome data in the FSP project has been slowed due to funding limitations.

The first quasiexperimental study gathered data from a sample of 215 offenders who were involved with FSP services from 1992 to 1993. Those involved with FSP (109 cases) were compared to an overflow group (106 cases) who had been on the waiting list and had received regular probation services only.

Offenders were considered a parole success in this study if they were still on parole one calendar year from the date of their release. Likewise, offenders were considered to have recidivated if they were rearrested and/or reincarcerated within one year of their release. In this study of a total of 215 cases with three missing cases, data from a t-test (p =.724, two tailed) and chi-square (.8845) both indicated no statistically significant differences between the comparison and FSP groups in terms of recidivism.

Although the findings between the FSP and comparison groups in terms of recidivism were not statistically significant, there is cause for optimism when further analysis is done on the completers vs. the comparison group. Those who completed FSP services had a 10% higher parole success rate than did the comparison group. This 10% difference in recidivism rates for persons completing a year of parole success means that for the total of 679 cases served by the project up to the end of 1993, an estimated 68 of the parolees may remain out of prison for a full year, at a potential savings of about $1 million to the state. In addition, 36 offenders who received some services and who successfully remained out of prison for one year saved the state more than $250,000 in prison maintenance costs alone. In addition, if one looks at the number of children and family members served by the two FSP groups who were successful—both the FSP completers and those who received some services—an estimated 150 children remained with their parents and families and were served as a result of the offender parent remaining in the community.

In addition, a second study has now been completed with follow-up data on those from the above 1993 FSP completer group (31 cases). Of those FSP offenders who completed FSP services and were planfully discharged, 67% (21 cases) remained in the community as of 1997 and had not been rearrested or charged. Thus, two-thirds of those who fully completed the program have now resided in the community successfully for four to five years. Although these data are from a small sample, they indicate the potential of FSP.

Conclusion

In the last decade, the overburdened criminal justice system has slowly begun to realize that incarceration does not eliminate the need for effective rehabilitation. While incarceration serves to relieve public concerns about safety, the fiscal burdens of incarceration demand that state officials seek other less costly and more effective preventive responses.

Likewise, the growing number of incarcerated adults has drawn attention to the children and families who are affected when family members are imprisoned. Children of incarcerated parents are at increased risk of out-of-home placement as well as intergenerational patterns of incarceration due to the increased poverty, trauma, and stigmatization, and inadequate quality of care that often accompanies the incarceration of a parent. These risks remain understudied.

The complex needs of offenders and their children and families cannot be addressed without the involvement of almost every human service system, including the criminal justice, child welfare, social service, educational, vocational and employment, mental health, and medical systems. Coordination of these efforts at the community level is crucial to enhancing the quality of services available, as well as to designing new services. The needs of this population and the obstacles to changing behaviors are much larger than those faced by most other service populations. The visible involvement of a school of social work and its university should indicate to social service agencies and the larger community the sense of priority that must be placed upon offenders and their families.

The social work profession can provide leadership in meeting these challenges by developing innovative programs for these populations. As the FSP program demonstrates, a holistic, community-based approach that provides community mobilization, advocacy, case management, and an array of individual and group services for offenders and their children and families can provide an alternative approach that is transportable to other communities. ◆

References

Adalist-Estrin, A. (1994). Family support and criminal justice. In S. Kagan & B. Weissbourd (Eds.), *Putting families first:America's family support movement and the challenge of change* (pp. 161–185). San Francisco: Jossey-Bass Publishers.

Adams, D., & Fischer, J. (1976). The effects of prison residents' community contacts on recidivism rates. *Corrective and Social Psychiatry, 22,* 21–27.

Bloom, B. (1995). Public policy and the children of incarcerated parents. In K. Gabel & D. Johnston (Eds.), *Children of incarcerated parents* (pp. 271–284). New York: Lexington Books.

Fishman, S. (1993). The impact of incarceration of children of offenders. In *Children of Exceptional Parents* (89–99). New York: Hawthorne Press.

Garbarino, J. (1992). *Children and families in the social environment.* New York: Aldine de Gruyter.

Gendreau, P. (1996). Offender rehabilitation: What we know and what needs to be done. *Criminal Justice and Behavior, 23*(1), 144–161.

Gendreau, P. (1994, November). What works in community corrections: Promising approaches in reducing criminal behavior. Presentation at IARCA Research Conference, Seattle, Washington.

Gilliard, D. K., & Beck, A. J. (1998). *Bureau of Justice Statistics bulletin: Prison and jail inmates at midyear 1997.* Washington, DC: U.S. Department of Justice, Bureau of Justice Statistics.

Hairston, C. (1988). Family ties during imprisonment: Do they influence future criminal activity? *Federal Probation, 52,* 48–53.

Hannon, G., Martin, D., & Martin, M. (1984). Incarceration in the family: Adjustment to change. *Family Therapy, 11,* 253–260.

Holt, N., & Miller, D. (1972). Explorations in inmate-family relationships. Sacramento, CA: California Department of Corrections.

Homer, E. (1979). Inmate-family ties: Desirable but difficult. *Federal Probation, 43,* 47–52.

Hostetter, E., & Jinnah, D. (1993). *Families of adult prisoners.* Washington, DC: Prison Fellowship Ministries.

Howser, J., & McDonald, D. (1972, August). Maintaining family ties. *Corrections Today, 11,* 96–98.

Johnston, D. (1995). Intervention. In K. Gabel & D. Johnston (Eds.), *Children of incarcerated parents* (pp. 199–236). New York: Lexington Books.

Jorgensen, J., Santos, H., & Warren, R. (1987). Addressing the social needs of families of prisoners: A tool for inmate rehabilitation. *Federal Probation, 8,* 47–52.

Kaplan, B., Cassell, J., & Gore, S. (1977). Social support and health. *Medical Care, 15,* 47–58.

Lauderdale, M. (1998). Stress and burnout phenomena in health and human service providers: The impact of changing paradigms. *Family and Community Health, 30*(2).

Lauderdale, M. (1998). *The survey of organizational excellence.* Austin, TX: The University of Texas Press.

Leclair, D. (1978). Home furlough program effects on rates of recidivism. *Criminal Justice and Behavior, 5,* 249–259.

Lynch, J. (1995). Crime in international perspective. In J. Q. Wilson & J. Petersilia (Eds.), *Crime* (pp. 75–89). San Francisco: ICS Press.

Martin, L. (1993). *Total quality management in human service organizations.* Newbury Park, CA: Sage Publications.

Phillips, E. L., Phillips, E. A., Fixsen, D., & Wolfe, M. (1974). *Teaching family handbook.* Lawrence, KS: University of Kansas.

Selber, K., Mulvaney, M., & Lauderdale, M. (1994, March). Innovations in faculty based field units: Bridges for university-agency partnerships. Annual Program Meeting, Council on Social Work Education. Atlanta, Georgia.

Selber, K. (1998). Challenges in measuring and managing quality in human service organizations. *Family and Community Health, 30*(2).

Sherif, M., & Sherif, C. (1965). *Problems of youth: Transition to adulthood in a changing world.* Chicago: Aldine.

Stark, R. (1987). Deviant places: A theory of the ecology of crime. *Criminology, 25,* 893–911.

Streeter, C., & Franklin, C. (1992). Defining and measuring social support: Guidelines for social work practitioners. *Research on Social Work Practice, 2,* 81–98.

Whittaker, J., & Garbarino, J. (1983). *Social support networks: Informal helping in the human services.* New York: Aldine.

Whittaker, J., Schinke, S., & Gilchrest, L. (1986). The ecological paradigm in child, youth, and family services: Implications for policy and practice. *Social Service Review,* 483–503.

The Forgotten Parent: Understanding the Forces that Influence Incarcerated Fathers' Relationships 8 with Their Children

Creasie Finney Hairston

Fathers who are in prisons and jails are not just convicts—they are parents as well. The family roles and responsibilities of incarcerated fathers, however, are seldom the focus of institutional policies, scholarly research, or child welfare services. This article examines the issues that must be addressed in designing policies and providing services that promote the maintenance of parent-child bonds and responsible parenting when fathers are incarcerated. It describes the family roles and structures of men in prison and looks at differences between public perceptions and the real-life experiences of prisoner parents. The ways in which correctional policies and child welfare practices influence and shape fathers' parenting abilities and father-child relationships are discussed, and strategies for creating a supportive environment for fathers and their children and families are proposed.

Creasie Finney Hairston, Ph.D., is Dean and Professor, Jane Addams College of Social Work, University of Illinois at Chicago, Chicago, IL.

Fathers who are in prisons and jails are not just convicts. They are parents too. They have the same dreams and aspirations for their children as other men and share some of the same parental commitments and obligations. Their children and families have expectations of them as well, although those expectations are frequently limited or altered by the realities of prison confinement. The family roles and responsibilities of incarcerated fathers, however, are seldom the focus of institutional policies, scholarly research, or child welfare services. Few family-oriented services are provided for incarcerated fathers or their children and father-child relationships are generally dismissed as irrelevant or simply ignored in broader efforts to strengthen families and promote children's welfare.

Several factors point, nevertheless, to the inclusion of incarcerated fathers as a useful and needed strategy in societal efforts to improve and enhance children's and families' well-being. Among these are the millions of children whose fathers are in prisons and jails, the millions whose fathers have been, or will be, incarcerated, and the millions more who will grow up while their fathers are in prison. Also important are our knowledge and understanding of the role of fathers in child development, of the negative impact of parental separation and paternal absence on children, and of the importance of regular parent-child contact in sustaining meaningful parent-child relationships during periods of separation [Gable 1992; Hairston & Lockett 1985; Jaffe 1983; Loar 1998]. The negative impact that the disproportionate number of African Americans in the prison population has on the communities from which those men come, and the resulting expectation of imprisonment as a part of the African American experience, is also a relevant factor in maintaining and supporting families [Moore 1996].

This article examines major issues that must be understood and addressed in designing policies and providing services that promote the maintenance of parent-child bonds and responsible parenting when fathers are incarcerated. It describes the family roles and structures of men in prison and looks at differences between public perceptions and the real-life experiences of prisoner parents. The ways in which correctional policies and child welfare practices influence and shape fathers' parenting abilities and father-child relationships are discussed, and strategies for creating a supportive environment for fathers and their children and families are proposed.

Family Status and Family Ties

National surveys of prison inmates provide excellent information on many aspects of prison operations and prisoner characteristics. Statistical reports disseminated annually advise, for example, that though prison numbers are escalating rapidly, certain social characteristics of the prison population have remained relatively constant over the past several years [McGuire & Pastore 1996]. Most prisoners are male, are young, have low levels of education, and are poor at the time of their arrest. Almost one-half of the U.S. prison population is African American, with African Americans constituting the majority of prisoners in some states [McGuire & Pastore 1996].

Information regarding family status and characteristics, in sharp contrast, is not readily available, with the most recent national data on prisoners' family status appearing in the *Survey of State Prison Inmates, 1991* [U.S. Department of Justice 1993]. Similarly, while scientific studies of prisons and prisoners abound, research on family roles and concerns, in general, and fathers' roles, in particular, are few and far between. The limited research on fathers in prison [Hairston 1989, 1995b; Koban 1983; Lanier 1987, 1993] and national survey data [U.S. Department of Justice 1993] that do exist, however, provide a picture of incarcerated fathers and their family relationships that is consistent across studies. At the same time, these research studies show marked contrasts with media images of prison populations and common assumptions about prisoners who are fathers. The discussion on prisoners' family status and relationships that follows is based primarily on the work of Hairston [1989, 1995], Koban [1983], and Lanier [1987, 1993].

Most men who are in correctional institutions are single or divorced. Fewer than a fourth are married. The number of fathers in prison is large and, consistent with a rapidly growing prison population, increases considerably each year. The majority are fathers of dependent children, for whom the fathers had some responsibility prior to incarceration. The percentage of imprisoned men with two or more children ranges from 40% [Hairston 1989] to 69% [Hairston 1995b]; the mean number of children per father is a little more than two.

Family networks are quite complex and changes in marital status and family makeup are rather common. Prisoners' lifestyles and family roles prior to imprisonment bear little resemblance to the prevailing view that impoverished African American men are absent from their homes and communities and occupy marginal family roles. Their lifestyles, however, also contrast strongly with traditional images of the American nuclear family.

The picture of a man and wife with one set of biological children does not describe the typical family structure of fathers in prison. Most incarcerated fathers are not currently and have never been married to the mother of one or more of their children [Hairston 1989, 1995; Lanier 1987]. Among those with two children, as many as 50% indicate the children have different mothers [Hairston 1995b]. The presence of different mothers holds for married, divorced, and single men.

Fathers have different provider and nurturing roles with their different children. Some of their children may have lived with them at the time of arrest, others were seen regularly, and still others were seen infrequently or not at all. Although unmarried, most men lived in the same household as at least one of their children (usually the youngest child) at the time of arrest. They contributed financially to that child's support and shared caregiving with the child's mother, who was also a household member [Hairston 1995b]. Many fathers also supported financially and/or saw regularly one or more of their children who did not live with them [Hairston 1995b; Lanier 1987]. These provider and caregiver roles were found among African American, Caucasian, and Latino fathers.

The parent-child relationships described here run counter to popular media images of prisoners generally and, more specifically, young African American males who constitute a large portion of the prison population. This picture of unmarried males involved and connected with their children differs markedly from negative stereotypes depicting deadbeat dads who produce children for whom they care little and provide nothing. The picture presented here is consistent, on the other hand, with the reports of several studies conducted over a period of years, and carried out in different locations and with different methodologies. Research studies of unmarried African American fathers show, for example, that substantial numbers spend time with their children, aid in their physical care, and have strong emotional attachments even when they do not, or are not able to, provide regular financial support [Barret & Robinson 1982; Freeman 1989; Laseter 1994]. Though emotional attachments and other forms of caring and concern are not substitutes for financial support or for the safety and security that fathers provide when children and parents live in the same household, they are, nevertheless, important to children and fathers and cannot be easily dismissed.

Parent-child relationships during imprisonment are tenuous at best. Most fathers in prison seldom see their children. Although fathers may receive information about their children from other family members, their own contact with their children during imprisonment is limited and dependent, to a large extent, on their ongoing legal relationship with each child's mother. Contrary to the common assumption that fathers are not cut off from their children as their wives willingly bring children for visits [Friends Outside 1986], fewer than one-third of fathers see at least one of their children on a regular basis [Hairston 1995b; Koban 1983; Lanier 1987]. While men who are married have visits more frequently with their children than single or divorced men, few men in prison, as previously noted, are married.

Parent-child relationships tied to marriage, though good while they last, are not secure and can't be counted on to continue. Marital relationships are severely strained and frequently terminate during imprisonment. Wives are seldom prisoners' most frequent visitors; in only 50% of cases are they prisoners' most important source of support [Hairston 1995b]. Stability in prisoners' family relationships centers around the prisoners' own mothers, who are their primary sources of encouragement, emotional support, information, and concrete aid [Hairston 1995b].

Fathers in prison care about their children and about how their children perceive them as fathers. Most fathers express concern for their children, worry about them, and worry about being replaced in their children's lives by someone else such as a stepfather [Hairston 1989, 1995b; Lanier 1987, 1993]. These worries are not unfounded, given the limited contact imprisoned fathers have with their children, the tense emotional bonds shared with their children's mothers and primary caregivers, and the absence of social supports for parenthood. Their concerns and worries appear to be genuine and not just socially desirable responses. Many readily acknowledge that they are not currently doing, or may not have done, the things a good father does. In addition, research demonstrates that their perceptions of themselves as fathers and of their father-child relationships are related to their own emotional well-being. Lanier [1993] found that the worse an incarcerated father's perception of his current relationship with his children, as measured by level of closeness, involvement, and contact, the more likely that the father experienced depression.

Obviously, there are some men of all classes and races who abandon their children and relinquish all responsibility for their care and upbringing. There are, at the same time, men of all classes and races who try hard to be a father to their children even during periods of separation and under the most difficult of circumstances.

Fathers who are in prison have some of the same concerns and difficulties as other fathers. While imprisonment, in and of itself, does not make them bad parents, it does present challenges and limitations that differ from those of other fathers separated from their children. When imprisoned fathers are viewed by families and the general public as unimportant to children, and when their parenting opportunities are narrowly prescribed or restricted to things they cannot do, they may withdraw or give up as fathers. Obviously there are limitations as to what fathers can do from prison, but considering their parenting roles in narrow, traditional ways more appropriate to resident fathers also lends itself to the curtailment or denial of services under the mistaken notion that services will do little good or that resources could best be used elsewhere.

Correctional Policies and Regulations

Parent-child relationships during imprisonment are not just dependent on personal preferences or family histories. Although they operate within the nexus of public opinion, public opinion is also not the sole determining factor. Imprisonment, in and of itself, presents major obstacles to the maintenance of family ties. Prisoners are not at liberty to see or talk to their children whenever they like. They cannot engage in their children's daily care, nor can they be present to assure their children's safety. They have no control over their own jobs or income and are not likely to have much to contribute to their families' financial support.

Contrary to official memoranda that cite the importance of family relationships to the achievement of correctional goals, prisons and jails are not family friendly and don't have a family orientation [Bauhofer 1987; Hairston & Hess 1989]. Prison inmates, not families, are the focus of correctional institutions, and punishment, security of the facilities, and safety of the individuals who work and reside there are the major priorities [Cripe 1997]. Helping fathers maintain relationships with their children is one of the least important considerations in day-to-day operations and is not a major consideration even in policies governing such areas as communication, work, and correctional fees, which are most relevant to family commitments [Hairston 1996].

Correctional policies, administrative regulations, and staff practices have a major influence on family relationships. Communication between prisoners and their children, whether by visits, phone, or mail, is highly regulated [Hairston 1996]. Rules frequently bear little relevance to correctional goals and are insensitive to family structures and needs. Policies among states vary widely, and within states, institutions have broad discretion with regard to communication practices. A pattern of restricting fathers' access to their children and erecting obstacles to the maintenance of father-child attachments is found across states [Hairston & Hess 1989].

Visiting

Visiting is particularly problematic. Access is limited by restrictions on the frequency, duration and time of visits; by requirements that denote children's mothers as the only ones who can escort children on visits or give them permission to visit; and by requirements that specify that a father must have documented proof that he is a child's biological father for the child to visit [Bauhofer 1987; Hairston 1996; Hairston & Hess 1989; Hairston et al 1997]. Obstacles to the maintenance of father-child attachments are imposed by restrictions on social interactions between parents and children during visits and by a focus on discipline and control of children without the provision of child-centered activities. In some institutions, for example, a parent may not hold a child on his lap. In others, a child's unruly behavior would be reason enough for the termination of a visit.

These restrictions and obstacles may be functional for the management of prisons. They are insensitive, however, to African American culture wherein family members, not just mothers, share responsibilities for childrearing, where fathers are not necessarily the "real" fathers, and where paternity is not always legally documented. It is not unusual in African American communities, for example, for men who share a household with a woman and her children to act as, and be known as, the father of the woman's children, though he is not their biological nor their legal father.

These restrictions also defy the reality of prisoners' family lifestyles. A father may have had children with different women, some of whom have no ongoing relationship or bond with the prisoner and see no need to spend a day with him in a prison visiting room. Visits between prisoners and women with whom they long ago severed ties are also not likely to occur because they could cause problems between the mother and her current mate, as well as between the prisoner and his current mate. Prisoners, not unlike other men, would have a hard time explaining to their current wives that their former girlfriends were visiting "only because of the children."

Prison visiting is both psychologically and physically demanding for children and adults as the visiting environment in most prisons is poor. Visitors are treated, at best, as unwelcome guests to be barely tolerated and, more often, as intruders to be kept in line through humiliation and intimidation [Bauhofer 1987; Hairston 1995a; Hairston 1996]. Standing in line for hours to be cleared for a visit that lasts less than half the time spent waiting, being subjected to pat and frisk searches and rude treatment, and visiting in crowded, noisy, dirty, overheated facilities, or with parents and children separated by a glass barrier, are hardly conducive to promoting family bonds. Only the most tenacious and committed families are willing or able to endure these conditions on an ongoing and regular basis.

It is relatively easy to see how some prisoners and families choose to forego regular visits to save themselves the embarrassment and helplessness associated with family contact under poor visiting conditions. The practical issue for fathers, however, is that parenting cannot be put on hold to be taken up "when I get out of prison." Children grow up; their memories fade or they create new ones through fantasy and imagination. When there is no contact to support an enduring bond, they begin to experience their parents as strangers. Such situations can lead to permanent, rather than temporary, severance of family ties.

Telephone and Mail Communication

The collect-call telephone policies that have made prison telephones a lucrative business for prisons and telephone companies also affect fathers' relationships with their children. At first glance, telephone contact seems like a good way to maintain relationships. Prison talk, however, is not cheap. The author's 1998 review of several families' phone bills indicated that a prisoner-initiated collect phone call costs the receiving household as much as three times more than had the call been placed collect from a pay phone by a person not in prison, and five to ten times more had the call been made from a residential phone. The incentives that phone companies make to attract residential customers don't apply to prisoners' calls to their families, as prisoners and their families are captive audiences who can be forced to pay maximum allowable rates.

Many prisoners' families are poor and unable to accept expensive collect phone calls on a regular basis. The author's numerous discussions with families and family advocates indicated that many families resent what they perceive as price gouging by phone companies and the correctional institutions who share the profits from prisoners' collect calls. Some families indicate that they restrict the number of calls or block all collect phone calls as their only recourse. Others accept calls though they generate family hostilities and open old wounds about the difficulties imprisonment and prisoners present for families. These calls, in addition, are hardly welcomed by children's mothers or other caregivers who do not have ongoing strong relationships with, or commitments to, the incarcerated fathers [Hairston 1996].

Communication by mail also carries social costs for families and children, as letters and packages from many prisons carry an external stamp denoting a warning that the letter is from a correctional institution. This public label makes many mothers and other caregivers discourage prisoners from sending mail to their homes. Though the caregivers may support children's relationships with their fathers, they prefer to do so in a way that is not stigmatizing to them. The personal stamp, like the operator announcing that a phone call is from a correctional institution, is a particular problem for those situations wherein a father's incarceration is a family secret.

Prison Wages and Child Support

Though communication is a critical area, it is not the only aspect of prison confinement that directly affects prisoners' parental obligations. Also relevant are prison wages and related issues of child support. Prison pay is generally meager and hardly enough to sustain prisoners, let alone any commitments they may have to contribute to their children's care. Most prisoners, whether they want to or not, are not in a position to carry out traditional paternal roles as financial providers. Their financial contributions are, at best, limited to purchasing or making handicraft gifts for holidays and birthdays. Some prisoners who work in prison industries (a minority of all prisoners) are able to send home small amounts infrequently to help with the ongoing upkeep of one of their children. The author's observations and discussions with prisoners and their families indicate, however, that most prisoners receive money from their families, who provide for their upkeep, rather than vice versa. This aspect of prisoners' financial status, however, has not stopped states' efforts to collect correctional fees from prisoners for doctor visits, health services, room and board, and back child support. Like the costs associated with exaggerated phone bills, however, these fees are collected at the expense of prisoners' families and children, thereby undermining not only family relationships during imprisonment but also hopes and opportunities for successful post-prison family environments, rehabilitation, and family reunification.

Child Welfare Practices

The maintenance of family ties is particularly challenging for incarcerated fathers when their children are involved in the child welfare system as wards of the state or as children at risk of placement. Fathers, in general, are not central figures in child welfare services and imprisoned fathers are easily dismissed by child welfare services as being uninvolved, inaccessible, and unlikely role models for children.

Although there is general recognition that the inclusion of parents (biological or psychological) is one of the most effective approaches for supporting children, fathers are usually neglected in child welfare services [Jaffe 1983; Lazar et al. 1991]: rarely are they acknowledged, accommodated, or supported; involved in decisionmaking about children; or included in planning, case plans, or service delivery. Even when fathers are considered, they are viewed as secondary caregivers, usually in terms of their financial support or nonsupport, or in terms of the problems they present rather than the resources they provide.

This neglect of fathers is also evident in family-oriented child welfare services such as family preservation, family reunification and kinship care. O'Donnell's [1995] study of kinship care, for example, showed that case workers had limited contact with fathers. They knew little about fathers' circumstances and did not collect the kind of information that would enable them to assess the fathers' potential for helping their children and identifying needed services. When workers did have contact with fathers, it was around the reasons for placement or the case workers' role. Fathers rarely participated in case planning or in administrative case reviews, though these service activities play a significant role in reunification, family maintenance, and permanency planning.

Incarcerated fathers occupy a position in child welfare that is even more marginal than other fathers. When fathers are sent to prisons and jails, most of their children do not enter the child welfare system as a direct result. Children whose parents are incarcerated are not highly visible [Hairston 1995b; Lanier 1987]. There are no national statistics to provide a picture of the nature and extent of this problem or of needed programs and services. There is little evidence that child welfare agencies have not identified parental incarceration as an issue of concern. Data on a father's status and whereabouts are not systematically collected and reported and information as basic as how many children in an agency's care have parents who are in prison is not known.

The author's review of child welfare policies from different states and Wall's [1997] report on an Illinois forum indicate that many state and local child welfare agencies do not have written policies regarding child welfare practice with incarcerated parents or have policies that are outdated, unknown to workers, specific to one institution, or relate to mothers only. Workers receive little or no guidance from agencies on relating to incarcerated fathers, as the topic is rarely covered in formal orientation, advanced training, or administrative manuals. Guidance is also not found in social work education or the scholarly literature, as few social work programs address criminal justice issues and social work and child welfare journals rarely have articles on the topic.

This absence of policies and administrative regulations to guide practice suggests that the agency-sanctioned approach to practice when children's fathers are incarcerated is to treat parental incarceration as an idiosyncratic or isolated event. Decisionmaking is left to the discretion of the individual worker to determine what, if anything, should be done to include parents in service planning [Hairston 1995a; Hairston et al 1996; Wall 1997]. Those workers who decide to involve incarcerated fathers in enhancing their children's welfare must do so without proper organizational supports. Those who don't forego opportunities to engage families in making informed decisions about the best interests of their children but are not likely to be adversely affected themselves.

Children's case workers are unlikely to receive inquiries or petitions from the fathers themselves or from anyone representing them. Some fathers don't know their children are involved in the child welfare system. Those who do may experience tremendous difficulty moving through the bureaucratic maze to identify and locate their children's case workers. Even when a father locates the case worker, there is little assurance that he will receive timely information, given the usual agency practices and procedures, the general neglect of fathers, and the difficulties workers experience in making contacts using typical correctional institution communication channels.

Correctional institutions and child welfare agencies do not have a history of collaboration that would support the maintenance of parent-child relationships when parents are in prison and children are wards of the state. The correctional focus on security and emphasis on punishment preclude the types of parental involvement and worker-client contact that the child welfare system requires for parents to demonstrate competent parenting to prevent the termination of parental rights and to promote family reunification.

The frequent father-child contact associated with successful family reunification is difficult when fathers are imprisoned, as is contact between fathers and case workers. Child welfare workers are subjected to the same rules as prisoners' other visitors; rarely are there established protocols giving child welfare workers professional courtesies for purposes of parent-child visits or information gathering and counseling sessions. Neither correctional institutions nor child welfare agencies place priority on seeing that prisoners are present at administrative case reviews and other hearings involving their children. In addition, neither correctional institutions nor child welfare agencies have in place established procedures or systems of accountability, such as liaison staff, or practice guidelines specific to incarcerated parenting to support mutual efforts.

Future Directions and Strategies for Change

A fundamental shift in ways of thinking about prisoners and their family roles, obligations, and commitments is needed to shape the development of family-oriented policies and programs when parents are incarcerated. The nature of the debate about children whose parents are incarcerated must be reframed to include fathers as important members of children's family networks. Whether fathers live in prisons or in neighborhoods, in households with or separated from their children, they have key roles in fostering their children's well-being. Children need their fathers and fathers need their children. Fathers need to feel that they are good parents and need to be supported in doing so.

Paternal involvement and connections with children and responsible fatherhood must occupy a more central position in any thinking about public policies, programs, and services. A public policy agenda with the goal of strengthening families should be broad and inclusive enough to embrace the millions of children and parents affected by parental incarceration. At the same time it is imperative that the unique challenges that imprisonment presents for parenting be recognized and that parental incarceration as a specific parenting and family public policy issue be addressed.

Notwithstanding the importance of individual case worker efforts and innovative parent support programs that operate in different locations, vision is needed at the highest policy and administrative levels to bring about and sustain fundamental changes. The major system forces that influence family attachments are not idiosyncratic or applicable only to a few prisons or jails or child welfare departments. Negative views about imprisoned men and their fathering roles are pervasive, as is the willingness of correctional institutions to disregard or severely restrict prisoners' family connections. Concerted leadership and goal-directed efforts are required for significant substantive changes that go beyond local communities or singular activities. Four basic strategies for creating the type and magnitude of change needed are offered here. While the focus is fathers, the recommendations also apply to incarcerated mothers and their children and to prisoner-family ties in general.

1. Child welfare and correctional leaders should establish national standards covering parents in prison and their children and adopt these standards as a part of the accreditation process for correctional institutions and child welfare agencies.

Standards and principles, such as those that cover prison industries and female offenders, set forth basic requirements for operating safe, humane, and effective service systems. When standards go beyond simply stating that an organization must have written rules (content and goals unspecified), they also provide frameworks for goals and operational policies and for significantly changing the nature of professional practice in a given area. They could, therefore, set the stage for a family-oriented and father-inclusive focus in corrections and child welfare.

Standards that promote a family orientation and support, rather than frustrate, incarcerated fathers' ability to carry out their parental roles and responsibilities are paramount for effecting change in correctional institutions. Those that acknowledge and address the special situations that parental incarceration creates for children in the child welfare system are similarly important in advancing child welfare goals. Standards that facilitate partnerships and professional exchanges between child welfare and correctional agencies in support of children and families are important to the broader criminal justice and social service communities.

In the past, the Child Welfare League of America and the American Correctional Association have provided leadership for standard-setting in their respective fields. Their leadership could be similarly applied here, not only for issues specific to their fields but also for forging mutual alliances and interprofessional task groups that address public interests when families are involved in both the criminal justice and child welfare systems. Both organizations have the status, prestige, and credibility crucial for successful change efforts that extend beyond a single organization or geographical area. Moreover, they have the infrastructure and resources to reach broad constituencies and to convene relevant groups and participants, including families and prisoners, to discuss the issues relevant to a national agenda.

2. State-level departments of child welfare and federal level child welfare agencies should provide leadership in developing model policies and administrative regulations to guide child welfare practice when children are involved in the child welfare system and their parents are in correctional institutions.

Family-oriented policy directives and agency protocols that are widely understood and practiced are required components of serious efforts to support parent-child relationships and promote children's well-being when parents are incarcerated. Policies guide the allocation of resources for training, visits, and parental contact; set the tone and context for parent-child communication; and demonstrate the relative value that states and agencies place on parent-child attachments. Moreover, they provide the organizational supports that staff need to engage families in client-centered, effective services, and set expectations and requirements for professional practice and organizational development. Agency protocols, developed in collaboration with corrections practitioners, can facilitate case worker contact with incarcerated parents, parent-child communication, and parental participation in meetings and hearings about the children.

Policies and protocols must be explicit with respect to fathers so that these men are not automatically excluded or subjected to benign neglect, as is too often the current practice. In addition, procedures should be in place to assure that policy implementation and day-to-day practices support agency goals without undermining parental rights, family preferences, or fathers' commitments.

3. Family advocates and child welfare and criminal justice professionals should promote the development of a national research, knowledge-building, and knowledge-dissemination agenda focusing on prisoners and their families and children.

The impact of parental imprisonment on prisoners' families and their children should be a priority area for research and policy analysis by national groups concerned with the public interest. Prisoners' ties with their children are relevant to family preservation and children's development, as well as crime prevention and recidivism. Despite the rapidly escalating number of children, families, and communities that are involved in the criminal justice and child welfare systems, there is no comprehensive database to answer even basic questions about prisoners' family status, childrens' needs, or successful programs and practices. There are, at the same time, many unanswered questions and untested assumptions about the impact of parental criminality and incarceration on children and about the impact of parent-child attachments and paternal responsibilities on adult recidivism. Research studies focusing on this area are scant, though information and knowledge to guide child welfare and corrections policies and programs are sorely needed.

Traditionally, federal agencies (i.e., the Administration on Children and Families, the National Institute on Justice) and national foundations have provided leadership for broad-based research programs by identifying a subject as a priority area, convening leaders in a field, and allocating funds for research and information dissemination activities. It is important that a broad-based constituency—social service providers, criminal justice practitioners, academicians, community leaders, prisoners, and families—be involved in defining research needs and approaches and in assessing and interpreting research findings and their implications for policy and practice. The "Dialogues on Child Welfare Issues" model for research dissemination and policy analysis, sponsored by the Illinois Department of Child and Families Services and the University of Illinois Jane Addams College of Social Work, is an exemplar for creating and sustaining an effective discussion forum among individuals and organizations with diverse interests and experiences [Hairston et al. 1997].

4. Social service organizations and practitioners should provide leadership for the development of public policies and service programs that help parents in prison maintain ties with their children and address family needs related to correctional supervision.

The Directory of Programs Serving Families of Adult Offenders [Family and Corrections Network 1992] lists a wide variety of program types and approaches operated under diverse auspices with different resources. They include community-based programs as well as those that operate in institutions. They include transportation services for prison visits, parent education programs, children's support groups, and children's visiting programs. No less important are advocacy and social reform projects that address deficiencies or areas of neglect in social services delivery and criminal justice processing. The basic theme reflected in these programs is that family services are needed at each stage of criminal justice processing and that the maintenance of parent-child bonds can and should be promoted during incarceration. Operating, to date, within the nexus of nonsupportive public opinion and public policies, they provide examples of accomplishments that can be made when there is caring and committed leadership in an area of social need.

Conclusion

Most incarcerated fathers care about their children and many try hard to be good parents against tremendous odds. The obstacles to the maintenance of parent-child relationships when parents are incarcerated are numerous, resulting from public policies, administrative regulations, and erroneous assumptions about fathers' connections with their children and children's needs for their parents. If there is a public will, however, systemic obstacles to maintaining family ties can be removed, without sacrificing security and safety in correctional institutions or the best interests of the children, without demeaning families or belittling and neglecting fathers, and without taking unfair advantage of vulnerable individuals to create institutional profits or operating funds. The establishment of standards and ways of working that are conceptually and practically sound and empirically valid, and that take into consideration the different values and goals in service and security-focused institutions, as well as the cultural backgrounds and family traditions of prison populations, can bring about significant positive changes.

In promoting responsible fatherhood among prisoners, it is not necessary to compromise family preferences, to romanticize ideal parent-child relationships that never existed, or to ignore parental behaviors that indicate that parent-child relationships or contacts are likely to be detrimental to children. It is critical to understand, however, that neither imprisonment nor engagement in illegal activities is synonymous with being a bad parent in the eyes of prisoners' children, their families, or their communities. Important as well is the understanding that the adults who make a difference for children and enable them to successfully handle life experiences are likely to be caring adults with whom they already share an emotional bond and attachment. It, therefore, behooves us to work diligently through policies, programs, and services to help fathers who are in prison help themselves and their children. Fathers who are in prison are parents too. ◆

References

Barret, R., & Robinson, B. (1982). Teenage fathers: Neglected too long. *Social Work, 27*, 484–488.

Bauhofer, V. (1987). Prison parenting: A challenge for children's advocates. *Children Today, 16*(1), 15–16.

Cripe, C. (1997). *Legal aspects of corrections management*. Gaithersburg, MD: Aspen Publishers, Inc.

Family and Corrections Network. (1992). *Directory of programs serving families of adult offenders*. Batesville, VA: Author.

Freeman, E. M. (1989). Adolescent fathers in urban communities: Exploring their needs and role in preventing pregnancy. *Adolescent Sexuality in Rural and Urban America*, 113–131.

Friends Outside. (1986). *Incarcerated mothers and their children*. Salinas, CA: Author.

Gabel, S. (1992). Behavioral problems in sons of incarcerated or otherwise absent fathers: The issue of separation. *Family Process, 31*, 303–314.

Gabel, S., & Shindledecker, R. (1993). Characteristics of children whose parents have been incarcerated. *Hospital and Community Psychiatry, 44*, 656–660.

Hairston, C. (1989). Men in prison: Family characteristics and parenting views. *Journal of Offender Counseling, Services & Rehabilitation, 14*, 23–30.

Hairston, C. (1995a). Family views in correctional programs. In R. Edwards & J. Hopps (Eds.), *Encyclopedia of social work* (19th ed.) (pp. 991–996). Washington, DC: NASW Press.

Hairston, C. (1995b). Fathers in prison. In D. Johnson & K. Gables (Eds.), *Children of incarcerated parents* (pp. 31–40). Lexington, MA: Lexington Books.

Hairston, C. (1996). How correctional policies impact father-child relationships. *Family and Corrections Network Report, 8*, 3–4.

Hairston, C., & Hess, P. (1989). Family ties: Maintaining child-parent bonds is important. *Corrections Today, 51*, 102–106.

Hairston, C., & Lockett, P. (1985). Parents in prison: A child abuse and neglect prevention strategy. *Child Abuse and Neglect, 9*, 471–477.

Hairston, C., Wall, N., & Wills, S. (1997). *Children, families, and correctional supervision: Current policies and new directions.* Chicago: University of Illinois at Chicago, Jane Addams College of Social Work.

Jaffe, E. (1983). Fathers and child welfare services: The forgotten client? In M. Lamb & A. Sagi (Eds.), *Fatherhood and family policy* (pp. 129–137). Hillsdale, NJ: Lawrence Erlbaum Associates.

Koban, L. A. (1983). Parents in prison: A comparative analysis of the effects of incarceration on the families of men and women. *Research in Law, Deviance and Social Control, 5*, 171–183.

Lanier, Jr., C. S. (1987). *Fathers in prison: A psychosocial exploration* (unpublished master's thesis, New Paltz College of the State University of New York).

Lanier, C. S. (1993). Affective states of fathers in prison. *Justice Quarterly, 10*, 49–65.

Laseter, R. (1994). *Young inner-city African American men: Work and family life* (unpublished doctoral dissertation, University of Chicago).

Lazar, A., Sagi, A., & Fraser, M. (1991). Involving fathers in social service. *Children and Youth Services Review, 13*, 287–300.

McGuire, K., & Pastore, A. L. (1996). *Bureau of Justice Statistics sourcebook of criminal justice statistics—1996.* Albany, NY: The Hindelang Criminal Justice Research Center, University at Albany.

Moore, J. (1996). Bearing the burden: How incarceration weakens inner-city communities. In Vera Institute of Justice (Ed.), *The unintended consequences of incarceration* (pp. 67–90). New York: Vera Institute of Justice.

O'Donnell, J. M. (1995). *Casework practice with fathers in kinship foster care* (unpublished doctoral dissertation, University of Illinois at Chicago).

Swan, A. (1981). *Families of black prisoners: Survival and progress.* Boston: G. K. Hall.

U.S. Department of Justice. (1993). *Survey of state prison inmates, 1991*. Washington, DC: U.S. Department of Justice, Bureau of Justice Statistics.

Wall, N. (1997). Policies affecting children whose parents are incarcerated. *Dialogues on Child Welfare Issues Report*. Chicago: Jane Addams Center for Social Policy and Research.

Wolozin, D., & Dalton, E. (1990). Short-term group psychotherapy with the family-absent father in a maximum security psychiatric hospital. *Social Work with Groups, 13*, 103–111.